REMEMBERING
NORRISTOWN

REMEMBERING

NORRISTOWN

STORIES FROM THE

Banks of the Schuylkill River

STAN HUSKEY

THE
History
PRESS

Published by The History Press
Charleston, SC 29403
www.historypress.net

First published 2009
Second printing 2009
All images courtesy of *The Times Herald* unless otherwise noted.

Manufactured in the United States

ISBN 978.1.59629.723.4

Library of Congress Cataloging-in-Publication Data

Huskey, Stan.
Remembering Norristown : stories from the banks of the Schuylkill River / Stan Huskey.
p. cm.
ISBN 978-1-59629-723-4
1. Norristown (Pa.)--History. 2. Norristown (Pa.)--Biography. I. Title.
F159.N7H87 2009
974.8'12--dc22
2009029925

To my wife, Sue, for her patience while I was writing this book.

CONTENTS

Introduction

When I first moved to the Norristown area in 1996, I have to admit that I wasn't too impressed with my surroundings. The town was run-down. There were boarded-up storefronts along Main Street and West Marshall Street, the two main shopping districts in the borough. Over the years, a quiet renaissance has been gaining momentum. A governmental housecleaning was in order, and it came to fruition in 2004, and during the ensuing years a slow but steady transformation from a down-in-the-mouth forgotten borough to a municipality on the verge of revitalization has taken place.

Norristown had been a borough since its inception in 1812 but changed its form of government to a municipality in April 2004, after a home rule charter study was commissioned and it was determined that the residents no longer wanted a mayor. Of course, the mayor was soon to be indicted, but that's another book in itself.

When I took that first drive heading east on Main Street to make my way to *The Times Herald* building and my job as a beat reporter, I had no idea that Norristown's history would begin unfolding before my very eyes on a daily basis. Norristonians are proud of their history, and they have every right to be. From the five Civil War generals buried in Montgomery Cemetery to the great jazz organist Jimmy Smith, Norristown has been the home of accomplished people from all walks of life throughout the ages.

After spending time as a beat writer covering the townships surrounding Norristown, I was assigned to the police beat, which meant that I was going to be spending a lot of time in Norristown from that point forward. While there were a number of people who told me how terrible Norristown was going to be, I immediately began to meet people who would prove them wrong.

Introduction

On one of my first days in Norristown, I met Frank Ciaccio, also known as Hank Cisco. He was on Ann Street handing out American flags with the help of Pearly Mae Robinson. Hank Cisco is a Norristown icon and has served as Norristown's ambassador since the mayor's position was eliminated in 2004. Many residents of Norristown will remember him as Sergeant Cisco, the friendly police officer who came into the town's elementary schools and taught them about safety. Others will remember him as the rough-and-tumble cop who didn't take any grief from anyone. Still others will remember him for the fighter he once was, yelling to him from across a street or busy store to "Keep bobbin' and weavin', Rock."

I met Charlie Tornetta, a mild-mannered gentleman who speaks fondly of his hometown. Like Ciaccio, his family hails from Sciacca, Italy, which is on the island of Sicily. The Tornetta family is known throughout the area for their real estate holdings, but they give back in so many ways to the community, albeit quietly. There is a large, proud Italian population in Norristown, as well as Irish and African American. The latest wave of immigrants hails from Mexico.

The Genuardi family started its grocery store chain in Norristown, growing it to a multistore conglomerate and spawning the Genuardi Foundation, which supports the town and the entire region, as does the Mirable family. The Mascaro family also goes quietly about its business of giving back to the community.

Later, I would meet Tom Lasorda, who spent his youth running the streets of the East End with the likes of Josh Culbreath and Jimmy Smith. While he is known for his years in baseball and taking Team USA to a gold medal in the 2000 Olympic Games in Sydney, Australia—beating a Cuban team that had won gold at the previous Olympic games—Lasorda also has spent a lifetime giving back to communities throughout the nation and the world.

The Italian community in Norristown rivals that of the Irish community, even though Italians immigrated to Norristown after the Irish and in fact used St. Patrick Church as their house of worship before establishing Holy Saviour. The Irish and Italian immigrants built Norristown from the ground up, with many of the Irish building the railroads that would bring goods into town and the Italians building the factories and mills that would employ a majority of the town's residents.

From its very beginning, Norristown thrived. Once the Town of Norris was established, the first mill was built at the end of Swede Street near the Schuylkill River. By the turn of the twentieth century, there were dozens of manufacturing plants throughout town. There were more than a dozen hotels and more than a dozen churches. The town was a transportation hub even then, with four train depots and the main highway for commerce between Philadelphia and all points west running right through the heart of town. There wasn't anything that couldn't be found in Norristown, and most of it was made right here. The population continued to grow throughout the years, reaching a peak of just under forty thousand in the mid-1900s. Today, more than thirty thousand people still call Norristown home.

Local residents will recall when then-Senator John F. Kennedy came to town. He stopped at the Valley Forge Hotel for a break before making his way on to Roosevelt Field to give a speech. President George Herbert Walker Bush came to Norristown Area High School in 1992, and then-Senator Barack Obama came to the George Washington Carver Community Center in 2005, long before he had announced his intention to run for president. He would return a few years later and drop in at the ShopRite in East Norriton to pick up a few items. Norristown Area High School also hosted President Bill Clinton while he was in office, quite a coup for a small suburban high school to have two sitting presidents pay them a visit.

Children's author Jerry Spinelli hails from Norristown, as does Major League Baseball's Mike Piazza. Peter Boyle, best known as Ray Romano's father on *Everybody Loves Raymond*, was from Norristown. Geno Auriemma, the head coach of the University of Connecticut women's basketball team, is proud to call Norristown home, as is Olympic great Josh Culbreath.

And the homes in Norristown are something to be seen. While not everyone lived in the magnificent structures that line the North End of town along DeKalb Street or the West End along Main Street, the architecture stands as a reminder to those who once did. There are a variety of architectural styles still visible throughout the town, even in the row homes and "twins" that make up a good portion of the housing in Norristown. There are mansions along DeKalb Street just north of Brown that are still well kept today. Unfortunately, most of the mansions along Main Street have been either torn down or divided into apartments or have been taken up by businesses of one form or another. Even so, the architectural detail is still visible and quite stunning. A drive through town will tell even the least curious that Norristown once was home to many wealthy individuals and families.

I'd like to thank Richard McDonough for taking the time to read over the manuscript for this book and John Fichter for lending me his copy of a Sanborn Map of Norristown and his book on Norristown from 1860.

In the pages that follow, you'll be taken on a journey through the history of a seemingly small town on the banks of the "hidden river" with a past as big as any city across the nation. Please take this brief history of Norristown and expand on it as needed. These pages are meant as a starting point for the twenty-first-century recording of the people and places that have made Norristown an incredible place to live and work.

PART I

NORRISTOWN'S HALCYON DAYS

Footsteps from days gone by seem to echo as you walk along Main Street in Norristown. The sight of a family strolling along the sidewalk in the early days of the twentieth century could easily have been the inspiration for a Norman Rockwell painting.

Norristown, the Montgomery County, Pennsylvania seat of government, was the place to be on a Saturday night. There were four movie theatres along Main Street in those days and shops and restaurants to satisfy every appetite. Main Street was originally called Egypt Street, named so because of the productiveness of the area. A cornerstone at the Fairmount Fire Co. attests to the original name of the street. Through the years, several movie houses lined Main Street. The Bijou was located at Main and Swede Streets and the Empire was at Main and Cherry Streets. The Lyric was on the north side of Main Street just below the public square, which was established when the courthouse was built in 1785. The Palace was at Main and Mill Streets and The Tower was located for many years at Main and Arch Streets.

While many were replaced with other venues through the years, perhaps the most memorable was the Norris Theatre. The Norris opened December 22, 1930, at 125 East Main Street with the movie *Fast and Loose*, starring Carole Lombard and Miriam Hopkins. The Art Deco style, designed by architect William Lee, was cutting-edge in its day. When the theatre was finally razed in 1983 to make way for a McDonald's, the twenty-foot-tall window grill façade was dismantled and taken to the Wolfsonian Museum in Miami, Florida. The McDonald's has since been torn down, and a new one was built at the corner of Main and Markley Streets, where the Wonder Bread factory once stood.

The Norris Theatre was a mainstay on Main Street in Norristown for many years. The façade is on display in a museum in Miami.

When the Norris Theatre opened, Norristown was one of the largest of Philadelphia's suburbs. The King of Prussia Mall was years away and the Blue Route had yet to be built. The streets were crowded with visitors from the four corners of Montgomery County nearly every weekday, but especially on Saturdays. The Norris Theatre was the last of the movie theatres to survive in Norristown. The opening of multiscreen theatres in nearby Plymouth Township and King of Prussia contributed to their demise. Harry Sablosky, attorney and secretary for the Sablosky Brothers, a group that operated most of the movie houses in Norristown, defended his need for finally selling out.

Norristown suffered the same fate as many other downtowns across America when malls quickly erased the allure of driving into town to shop. The King of Prussia Mall, which rivals the Mall of America in Minnesota, opened in 1963, but Norristown hung on for a few more years after that with a large variety of specialty shops that had a large following of devoted patrons.

The "Biggest Borough in the World" quite easily could have been described as the original "City of Broad Shoulders," considering the industrious nature of the town. From the mid-1800s to the mid-1900s, Norristown continued to grow in population and stature. Ironworks were common throughout and kept many men employed for many years. Mills and factories drew people to the town for employment. There were tack factories, shoe factories and more than a dozen mills, along with three cigar factories and a shirt factory. The W.K. Gresh & Son's Cigar Factory, which once employed more than one thousand people, still stands today and has been converted into an apartment building. The Tyson Shirt Factory, which started out as the Quaker City Shirt Manufacturing Company, was recently renovated as well and is an apartment building adjacent to the cigar factory. Tyson once employed about one thousand employees.

The Adam Scheidt Brewing Company was located off Markley Street, with the front entrance just a block east on Marshall Street. The brewery changed hands and was later called Schmidt's Valley Forge brewing company. The administration building still stands at Marshall and Barbadoes Streets and has been converted into office space.

Schall's Iron Works was at the intersection of Markley and Washington Streets, and the Norristown Iron Works plant was at the corner of Washington and Barbadoes Streets. But the major employers in town were undoubtedly the mills. Globe Knitting Mills was located on Main Street and Wyoming Spinning Company and Eureka Knitting Company were in the same building at the bottom of Swede Street. The Herbert Hosiery

The window of Wilson's Pharmacy was used for a Welch's grape juice display around the turn of the twentieth century. *Courtesy of Jim and Pat Wolf.*

Mill was at Washington and Noble Streets and the Norristown Dress Co. was at 225 West Marshall Street. The Rambo and Regar knitting mill building still stands today on East Main Street and has been converted into offices for the Gretz Beer Co., which took over from the Mirable family just a few years ago.

Norristown was self-sufficient. There wasn't anything that anyone needed that couldn't be found within the borough's borders. The storefronts along Main Street once were filled with clothes, shoes and sundry other items. Chatlin's and Block's were the two major department stores in town, and they were surrounded with a variety of specialty stores that catered to the residents' every need. Gilberts, the men's store, was on Main between Cherry and Barbadoes Streets. Pagel's Clothing was at 36 East Main Street. Lou Belle was at 50 East Main Street and the W.T. Grant Co. was just a few doors down at 58 East Main Street. Morris Jewelers and Lanz Jewelery were both in the first block of East Main Street, along with the Sun Ray variety store, and Sears Roebuck and Co. was located at 227 West Main Street before it moved out to Logan Square. Kahn's furniture store was located at 134 West Main Street. There was an Acme supermarket at DeKalb and Marshall Streets, and the A&P was at 815 DeKalb Street, while the Food Fair could be found at Main and DeKalb Streets. Norristown was a commercial destination for many of the suburban towns outside Philadelphia. During Norristown's halcyon days, there wasn't an empty storefront to be found.

As commerce grew at a rapid pace downtown, other parts of Norristown were served by local markets, the precursor of the convenience store. Marshall Street evolved into a thriving business district on its own, supported by the large number of people working in the cigar factory and the shirt factory. On the north end of town, Logan Square, at the corner of Markley Street and Johnson Highway, was home to the "Ports of World." Sears was located there for many years and unveiled what is believed to be the first escalator in its store.

Norristown had it all, according to noted author Jerry Spinelli, who makes a guest appearance later in this book.

"Norristown was a city with an international flair," is the way track icon Josh Culbreath describes the town when he recalls his youth and run for the gold in Oslo, Norway, and Melbourne, Australia, later in these pages.

Norristown's most famous bibliophile, Charles Blockson, recalls growing up in Norristown with mixed emotions. The people were of all walks of life, but segregation always seemed to be in the air, Blockson said.

Norristown's Halcyon Days

The storefronts today are mostly filled with mom and pop stores, nail salons and Chinese takeout restaurants. But things are changing once again in Norristown. There are stalwarts on Main Street that simply won't let the bad times overtake the spirit of this once proud town, and the feeling of a renaissance is almost palpable. Two new parking garages, one at Main and Cherry Streets and the other adjacent to the transportation center on Lafayette Street at the corner of DeKalb Street, have been built in the past few years, and new sidewalks and façades have been put in place along DeKalb Street north of Marshall Street. The current council is hard at work establishing an Avenue of the Arts, and the Montgomery County Cultural Center is working with a group to establish a new home for its theatre group, which is located on DeKalb Street in the heart of the proposed Avenue of the Arts. Grant money has been secured to replace the sidewalks on DeKalb Street from Lafayette to Marshall, where new sidewalks already have been installed. As a side note, DeKalb Street was named for the German baron Johan DeKalb, who died fighting for the colonies in the Revolutionary War.

A development company has taken over portions of Logan Square, and a movie studio is planned for the site. In early 2008, the sale of the twenty-five-acre Logan Square shopping center was made final. Develcom, out of Bellmawr, New Jersey, purchased the property and has secured a $10 million grant to build the studio. Production was expected to begin in the early part of 2009, but the plans have been altered during the past year, and it is still unclear when the Studio Centre at Norristown will begin making movies.

Norristown is on its way back, but at the turn of the twentieth century, it was already there. On the 100th anniversary (1912) of the founding of the Borough of Norristown, Samuel Stephens, of Stephens Music House on West Main Street, penned "Dear Norristown." A copy of the original score was brought to *The Times Herald* by John Kehoe of Pine Street and was printed in the May 3, 1962 edition, which celebrated Norristown's sesquicentennial.

"Dear Norristown"
Words and Music by Samuel Stephens

This lovely month of May when grandeur holds full sway,
The sun shines brightly from the skies above
Dear Norristown serene, the fairest ever seen,
Where nature dwells with happiness and love,

The Adam Scheidt Brewing Company was located off Markley Street, with the front entrance just a block east on Marshall Street.

Norristown's Halcyon Days

One hundred years ago the town began to grow,
It's now the greatest borough in the land
Old friends so fond and true, we've open arms for you,
And glad to greet you with a welcome hand.
Home, home, sweet home, how I love that sweet refrain,
Oh it fills my soul with joy to meet dear friends again,
Should old acquaintance be forgot be they humble or renowned,
We welcome each and ev'ry one to dear old Norristown.

My childhood happy days are deep within my heart,
Those youthful mem'ries ever dear to me,
The morning glories twined around the cottage door,
'Twas there my mother took me on her knee,
Fancy I can see the mill-wheel turning round,
The little old log cabin in the lane,
The church and village school, the spreading chestnut tree,
Oh how I wish those days would come again.

Home, home, sweet home, how I love that sweet refrain,
Oh it fills my soul with joy to meet dear friends again,
Should old acquaintance be forgot be they humble or renowned,
We welcome each and ev'ry one to dear old Norristown.

Let echoes from the hill of dear old Valley Forge,
Lend forth their grandeur as our voices rise,
Let music fill the air and flags float ev'ry where,
As we go marching under azure skies,
Dear Norristown so gay, we celebrate this May
The hundredth anniversary of your birth,
Oh ring ye merry bells and peel forth loud and long,
And sing to all the world your welcome song.

Home, home, sweet home, how I love that sweet refrain,
Oh it fills my soul with joy to meet dear friends again,
Should old acquaintance be forgot be they humble or renowned,
We welcome each and ev'ry one to dear old Norristown.

Nearly one hundred years later, Norristown has suffered the fate of many downtowns across the nation. When the King of Prussia Mall was built, followed by the Plymouth Meeting Mall in Plymouth Township and even the mall in Montgomery Township, searching for parking spaces in downtown Norristown and walking for blocks just to get to a store was no longer appealing to the masses. As a result, stores downtown began to fade away by degrees; Gilberts was perhaps the last of the old stores to hang on. However, I would be remiss not to mention at least one of the businesses that have survived not only the onslaught of the mall, but also the "big box" home improvement stores: Zummo's Hardware. Zummo's is a throwback to days gone by. When you walk in, you're treated to personal service and an air of nostalgia.

That same air can be found inside Lou's, just east on Main Street from Zummo's. While the sandwich shop can't lay claim to inventing the zep, Norristown's very own creation, it can lay claim to making one of the best around. Linfante's, once located on Main Street, is generally credited with creating the zep, which basically is a hoagie without lettuce that is served on a round roll.

When the Pennsylvania Turnpike was being planned, Norristown's powers that be wanted nothing to do with it, and the town was literally passed by. However, with the improvements mentioned above and with other plans on the drawing board, Norristown is poised to take advantage of the "downtown" renaissance taking place all across America.

Settling by the Schuylkill River

When settlers arrived at a spot on the banks of the Schuylkill River that would one day become known as Norristown, Lenni-Lenape Indians were already calling it home. The Lenni-Lenape were part of the great Algonquin nation. The Unamis, or Turtle tribes; the Unalachtgos, or Turkey tribes; and the Monseys, or Wolf tribes, made up the Lenni-Lenape that called this area home.

The Dutch, Welsh and English, mostly Quakers, were the first to arrive in this area around 1616. Once here, they dubbed the river that sustained them the Schuyl-Kill, which means concealed, or hidden, river. A path near the banks of the Schuylkill eventually became known as Egypt Street and later Main Street in Norristown and Ridge Pike east and west of the municipality. "The Ridge," as it is known to locals, was the path traveled from Philadelphia through Norristown and to points west.

William Penn is said to have bought the land where Norristown now stands from the Lenni-Lenape in June 1684, about a year after he founded

Philadelphia, although no documents can be found to indicate the price he paid. In 1704, Penn gave his son, William Penn Jr., a tract of land called Williamstadt Manor, consisting of about seven thousand acres. That land would later be called Norriton, which then comprised what are now Norristown, East Norriton and West Norriton. The younger Penn is said to have sold the land five days later to Isaac Norris and William Trent, two Philadelphia merchants, for £850. Trent sold his share to Norris in 1712 for £500 and moved to New Jersey, where he settled what would become known as Trenton.

When Isaac Norris bought Trent's share of the land, he immediately built a gristmill at the foot of what is now Swede Street. Log houses were built nearby for those working in the mill, and in 1730, a decree from Philadelphia established Norriton Township. The town that would eventually become known as Norristown, carved from the southern corner of Norriton Township, was always shy one resident—Isaac Norris never lived in the town named for him.

Isaac Norris died on June 4, 1735. He left his land to his son Charles. After Charles's death in 1771, his widow auctioned off 543 acres of land that is now the center of Norristown, at the time known as Norrington, for £4,270. The tract of land was destined to change hands yet again. Colonel John Bull bought the land in 1771 for £4,600 and sold nearly all of it in 1776 (keeping 55 acres for himself) for £6,000 to Dr. William Smith, provost of the College and Academy of Philadelphia, which later would become the University of Pennsylvania.

When Montgomery County was established in 1784, Smith dispatched his son into the new county to establish the Town of Norris, which would become the county seat. The town was laid out by Smith's son, William Moore Smith. It covered a mere twenty-nine acres and had only sixty-four lots. The boundaries would have been what are today from Cherry Street to Green Street, heading west to east, and from Lafayette Street to Airy Street, heading south to north. Egypt Street, which is now Main Street, and Airy Street were the only real streets at the time; the others were nothing more than alleyways.

The selling and reselling of Norristown wasn't quite finished. Under Smith, the University of Pennsylvania sold its holdings to Smith's son, William Moore Smith, in 1791, who then sold to John Markley in 1802. Included in both sales was Barbadoes Island, which consisted of eighty-eight acres. Barbadoes Island is now part of West Norriton Township, and has been since Norriton Township was divided. Under the agreement, a tract of land on the side south of the courthouse was to remain open in perpetuity; it soon became known as the public square. The square is still open to the public today. It was dedicated as Hancock Square in July of 2008, named after the Civil War hero, Winfield Scott Hancock.

Before Egypt Street (later Main Street) was much more than a dirt path, plans were underway for the development of the Schuylkill River. It is believed that the plans for the first canal ever constructed in the United States were laid right here in Montgomery County. However, that canal was never completed.

David Rittenhouse, a leading scientist in his day, was one of the first to study the idea of using canals to move boats up the river where the water became too shallow. Rittenhouse, who was actually born in Germantown but moved to Norristown with his parents when he was just two years old, was studying the idea before the Revolutionary War, and he wanted to connect the upper branches of the Schuylkill River with the Susquehanna River and on to the Delaware River.

In 1793, the Schuylkill Canal Navigation Company, founded by Rittenhouse, William Moore Smith, Elliston Perot, Cadwallader Evans Jr. and Francis Jackson, began selling stock in the company at $200 a share.

General Andrew Porter, who served with distinction in the Revolutionary War, was appointed general manager of the new venture at a salary of $1,200 a year. By August 1793, Porter had 175 men working on the canal, with heavy excavation work taking place near the shore of the river at Swede Street. The crews worked through the next two summers, but the canal was still incomplete. The company appealed to Philadelphia for additional funding, as it already had spent $400,000, and reasoned that the canal would be a benefit to the city. Talks went on for several years, but work on the canal ceased. The company also appealed to the state legislature, which approved a lottery in an attempt to raise money. But the plan eventually failed, and the legislature ordered the company to merge with the Susquehanna Canal Company to form the Union Canal Company. The new company continued the lottery for many years. It enjoyed some success along the upper part of the Schuylkill River, above Reading, but no barges ever passed through the section in Norristown. It wasn't until 1824 that enough of the river had been channeled to make it passable from Port Carbon in Schuylkill County to Philadelphia. By this time, Norristown was fed up with the canal business and asked that any excavating be done on the south side of the river.

Norristown's Halcyon Days

Once the county was established, the Town of Norris began to grow. The first county courthouse was built in 1785 and a prison was built the following year. By 1790, there were three inns and seventeen houses in town, along with a store and a gristmill. The population stood at about 100. By 1820, the population had grown to a mere 827 people, but the completion of the canal along the banks of the Schuylkill River opened the proverbial floodgates.

The Town of Norris was soon to become a hub of commerce. The DeKalb Street Mill opened in 1836, Eagle Iron Works in 1838, Derr's Marble Works in 1842 and Hooven's Iron Mills in 1846. Thirteen stagecoaches were passing through Norristown to Philadelphia on a daily basis by 1830, and the population rose to 2,937 by 1840 and doubled the following decade to 6,024. Today, Norristown's population stands at about 31,000, down several thousand from the days when it seemed to be bursting at the seams.

While Norristown is struggling to remake itself today, it is not the first time the municipality has fallen on hard times. The following is an excerpt from *Directory of the boroughs of Norristown and Bridgeport* by William Whitehead, published in 1860.

Though somewhat depressed by the financial crisis which gave a check to trade within the last few years, Norristown is slowly, but effectually recovering from its depression; her recuperative energies, in a brief period, will be so thoroughly aroused, as to insure a rapid and continuous development of all her business departments, and a corresponding enlargement of area. It is impossible for such a community, possessing skill, wealth and intelligence, with a host of appliances which tend to prosperity, to suffer long from monetary embarrassment.

Situated in one of the most productive vallies of the world, and directly in the channel of its already great and increasing trade; with the rare advantages derivable from three rail roads, a canal, and a river that furnishes unfailing power for the propulsion of machinery; it would be a most unwarrantable conclusion to assert that she can remain in a stationary condition. Every dam upon her great water course has arrested the tide of population, gathered upon its borders the nucleus of a city, and stimulated every branch of human industry. The immense fields of coal upon the head waters of the Schuylkill, where thousands of toiling sinews search their leads, and constantly heave their dark masses to the surface, whence are fed continuous streams of trade; the hills which mark its course and from which large deposits of iron, lead, marble, limestone, slate and sandstone are daily drawn; with the products of the farm, the forge, the rolling mill, the machine works, the foundry, the loom, and numerous other pursuits, give a never ceasing impulse to skill, and make the entire valley a scene of unrivaled animation and energies. All of these ramifications of business have told with wonderful effect upon the valley, in lining the shores with an ever busy population, contributing to the every want and comfort of life. The connection of Philadelphia and Norristown by one continuous street, is by no means a wild vagary of the brain.

Norristown had it all, and nothing could keep it down. Egypt Street connected the borough to the great city of Philadelphia, ensuring its commercial success, and being the county seat meant a steady stream of visitors from all parts of the county. While industry has left Norristown behind, commerce is still intact, albeit in much smaller numbers, and the courthouse still ensures that steady stream of visitors.

Norristown's Namesake—Isaac Norris

One would think that the man after whom the town was named might actually have taken up residence here at one time or another, or perhaps even slept in a bed or two, a la George Washington, but history tells us otherwise. Isaac Norris never lived in Norristown, which was known as Williamstadt Manor when he purchased the land and later as Norrington before Norristown was established.

Isaac Norris was born to Thomas Norris in London on July 26, 1671, and the family migrated to Jamaica around 1678. As a young man of just twenty-one years, Isaac Norris, a Quaker, was in Philadelphia on business when a major earthquake struck the West Indies and his entire family was killed. Norris moved to Pennsylvania with very little money in his pocket and found success. He and a business partner, William Trent, bought a large parcel of land, called Williamstadt Manor at the time, from William Penn's son, William Jr. Norris bought out his partner soon after, leaving him in possession of all the land that would eventually become Norristown and East and West Norriton. Norris also purchased several hundred acres in the Northern Liberties section of Philadelphia, where he built Fair Hill, the family's estate. Norris eventually became mayor of Philadelphia and a judge in the Court of Common Pleas. He was offered a seat on the Pennsylvania Supreme Court but turned it down. Norris did become speaker of the Pennsylvania General Assembly. He died in 1735. There is scant evidence to suggest that Norris ever spent time in Norristown.

Suburban Philadelphia, to Norris, stretched only out to the northern boundaries of the city. When Norris had purchased property in the Liberties section, then outside Philadelphia, he was also granted a tract of land in the city, which is where his son Charles lived. Another of Isaac's sons, also named Isaac, would take over at Fair Hill after his father's death and live there the remainder of his years.

From Norris to Norristown

The Town of Norris, which was carved out of Norriton Township, was the first official name of the "Biggest Borough in the World." When the county was established in 1784, the Town of Norris was established soon after and would later be designated the county seat.

Things could have turned out much differently, however, as residents of the western edge of Philadelphia County were looking to start a new county west of Perkiomen and Skippack Creeks, with Pottstown being the county seat. The Pennsylvania Assembly voted against the idea but appointed a commission to study the possibility of creating a new county out of a portion of Philadelphia County. The population in the Norristown area was growing rapidly, and residents were complaining about the long trek into Philadelphia to attend court when necessary.

By March 1784, the commission returned with the recommendation that a new county be established with the boundaries extending from the Delaware River to the Schuylkill River, and from south of Germantown, with the county seat being somewhere near where Stony Creek flowed into the Schuylkill River. This didn't sit too well with the residents of Germantown and Chestnut Hill, and the boundaries were altered to start the new county west of Chestnut Hill. The final bill was passed on September 10, 1784, and the state had its fifteenth county.

Before the courthouse was built, court was held usually in taverns, with the paperwork being tended to in the homes of Colonel Craig or Frederick Muhlenberg in Trappe. The earliest records of any county business are from the recording of a deed by Muhlenberg on October 19, 1784. As of yet, no county business was recorded in the Town of Norris.

On December 1, 1784, Muhlenberg presided over the first orphans' court, also in Trappe, and a session of the court was held December 28, with five justices of the peace making up the court. County offices were established and a grand jury was convened, with Muhlenberg charging the jury. The next day, a session of common pleas court was held, but it is unclear where the court was actually located. Minutes indicate that the court was held at "the house of John Shannon," and "house" usually meant a tavern. If so, the court sessions were most likely held at the Barley Sheaf tavern on Germantown Pike, which today is in East Norriton Township. While Shannon was recognized as the landlord of the tavern, oddly enough, there are no official court records to indicate that he owned the property. A later recording shows Shannon purchasing a farm on the west side of Stony Creek but it does not indicate a tavern. By September 1785, records indicate that court sessions were now being held in "Norris Town," even though construction of the courthouse was not yet complete.

County court would continue to be presided over by justices of the peace until 1790, when the state constitution was amended "to have a man learned in the law preside as president judge." Muhlenberg presided as president judge until 1785, when he was succeeded by James Morris. But he retained the offices of recorder of deeds and register of wills until 1789, when he and his brother, General Peter Muhlenberg, were elected to the first House of Representatives. Frederick Muhlenberg was then chosen as the first Speaker of the U.S. House of Representatives.

While being referred to in some cases as Norris Town, the Town of Norris was its official name until the borough of Norristown was established on March 31, 1812, when Governor Simon Snyder signed a charter granted by the state legislature. However, an election was needed for a burgess, a constable and seven councilmen. The first official day of the borough of Norristown was May 1, 1812. Minutes from that first day of official business include an accounting of the election:

> *At an election held at the Court House in Norristown on Friday the first day of May A.D. 1812 for the purpose of electing officers for the Borough of Norristown. The following persons were duly elected to the offices annexed to their respective names, to wit: For Burgess—Gen. Francis Swaine. For Town Council—John Coates, Philip Hahn, Lewis Schrack, Robert Hamill, David Thomas, Mathias Holstein, James Winard. High Constable—Wendell Fisher.*

Norristown politics being what it is, it is interesting to note that the first burgess of Norristown, General Francis Swaine, was the son-in-law of Henry Melchior Muhlenberg, whose son, Frederick, who, as stated above, was the first Speaker of the U.S. House of Representatives.

From the day of the first election, Norristown has taken its place in history, and the people of Norristown have been proud of the town they call home, defending it throughout the years with a sense of pride. The first action taken by the new council was to have "the town clerk keep and possess the common seal." Norristown politics being what it is, once again, it is interesting to note that it would take Norristown twenty-one years to come up with a common seal. The beehive that adorns Norristown's seal was the creation of William Kneass, an engraver and die-maker for the U.S. Mint. Above the beehive are the words "Fervet Opus," and around the outside of the seal is simply stated, "The Borough of Norristown— Incorporated March 31, 1812." *Fervet opus* is Latin for "the work boils" and has been loosely translated over the years to mean that Norristown is a busy place.

In 2004, Norristown officially became a municipality, losing the borough moniker it had held for more than 190 years.

From the beginning, Norristown seemed on a path of continual growth, although the population grew rather slowly during the first few decades. Census figures show Norristown's population at 827 in 1820 and at 1,089 by 1830. A century later, Norristown had a population of 35,853.

After the first courthouse was built in 1785, construction was in perpetual motion. The first county prison was built a year later. Before the original courthouse was torn down, the original county prison was razed, but only after a new prison was built just across Airy Street, where it still stands today. The county uses it mainly for storage these days, but there is talk of using the intimidating structure for some type of artistic endeavor or cultural attraction. Locals will recall the young boys who would stand outside the prison waiting for a homemade baseball to be hit over the wall.

A public library was established in 1794 and has grown to serve the entire county. The Montgomery County Norristown Public Library is now located at Swede and Powell Streets. Just a few years later, the *Norristown Gazette* published its first issue on June 15, 1799. This forerunner of *The Times Herald* has been in constant publication ever since and is considered to be the thirteenth oldest newspaper in the country. At one time, Norristown

The "old" county prison was actually a new one back in 1787, when the first county prison was razed to make room for the county courthouse.

was home to three daily newspapers. The *Register*, founded in 1800, later disbanded, and the *Times*, founded in 1881, merged with the *Norristown Herald*, forming the *Norristown Times Herald* in 1922.

The first school was established in 1805, and although there are records showing public schools in Norristown before that date, legislation made way for the first academy in Norristown. State legislation that created the public school system as it is known today was enacted in 1834. When it was proposed, it was met with stern opposition from residents who were concerned that their taxes would be raised to educate students and to build new schools, and from residents who didn't have children. The same arguments remain today.

Each municipality throughout the state voted on the school legislation, which was optional at the time, and Norristown voters approved the new system in 1835. Almost twenty years later, the office of superintendent was created. In 1854, Dr. Ephraim Acker, at the time the publisher of the Norristown *Register*, was appointed the first superintendent for Norristown schools.

A fact that many readers will not find surprising is that one of the first acts of the new Norristown government was to levy a tax on its residents. Records indicate that the borough collected $317.86 in taxes in its first year and spent only $239.57, thus recording a surplus of $77.29.

The first wharf was built on the Schuylkill River in 1814, which was important for the commercial growth of the town because most goods were transported on the river. Swedes Ford was the major crossing point of the river until 1829, when a wooden bridge was built, linking Norristown to Bridgeport and destinations south.

The first train reached Norristown in 1835 on tracks that would become the Reading Railway, and the Industrial Revolution was about to begin. Before the railroad, Norristown had to ship goods by stagecoach or on boats along the river. The railroad took over for both, leading to the demise of both means of exporting and importing before long. Two trains a day made their way to and from Philadelphia, with passenger service costing thirty-seven cents. The first depot was at DeKalb and Washington Streets, not far from where the Norristown Transportation Center is today.

The first telephones in Norristown connected the Norristown Hose Company, which was located on DeKalb Street between Airy and Marshall Streets, with a livery stable on DeKalb Street just below Lafayette Street in 1878. Wires were strung along the rooftops of buildings between the two, and when the first call was made, crowds gathered at both locations to be part of history.

Norristown's government would remain constant for many years to come. As the borough prospered, there was no reason to think that any form of government would work any better, although there were attempts through the years to "upgrade" Norristown's status to that of a city.

However, after hard times began to fall on the county seat, a move to alter the borough's home rule charter was successful in 1986, when the mayor's position attained much more power (some would say entirely too much) in an effort to relegate council to that of a legislative body. Less than two decades later, in 2004, Norristown's government was once again in turmoil. The mayor's position was a vehicle to simply run roughshod over government workings. Norristown was falling into debt. A state takeover seemed imminent. The council commissioned a home rule charter study, headed by a former mayor, William DeAngelis, who admitted that the mayor's position had become too powerful. With mounting debt, the council moved to eliminate police officer and firefighter positions, a very unpopular move in a town that was struggling with crime. The following is an account that appeared in *The Times Herald* describing the political atmosphere and fiscal position of the borough in 2004:

> *They shed the term "borough" like they shed the office of mayor in April when they changed the Home Rule Charter to eliminate the mayor's position. Becoming a municipality was perhaps a mere side effect. Supporters said the change would bring Norristown in line with neighboring, wealthier townships, which have township supervisors to decide local code. Opponents said it was a backdoor attempt by a council at odds with the mayor to get rid of him for the sake of public expediency. Even Mayor Ted LeBlanc, whose role is now mostly ceremonial, contends that the vote effectively amounted to a recall. The roots of the change date back at least 18 years. Since borough residents last altered the Home Rule Charter—the borough law that governs local officials—the office of the mayor has been controversial. That was in 1986. The mayor's position was originally designed to counteract the power of a council that had direct input into the workings of a department. If you wanted your street paved, you had to see the councilman in charge of public works, which resulted in griping about who got "special favors." The mayor's office changed that. Council was relegated to a legislative role. A series of opinions by successive local solicitors gave the office more power. In 2002, a long-running fight with the mayor over the budget passed a deadline*

and by default forced the adoption of the mayor's budget. Council had little control over spending. The result was years and years of budget deficits, including trips to the Montgomery County Court House to borrow millions of dollars to cover the year-end debt. In 2003, council and the mayor were forced to ask a judge for permission to borrow $4.13 million from a judge who in 2002 told them not to come back. Even one of the architects of the 1986 charter, Bill DeAngelis—himself a former mayor—agreed that the mayor's position was unwieldy. He, along with other former borough officials, helped write the new charter after being elected to the Government study commission. It was a process that took at least a year. They sent it to the voters April 27. LeBlanc filed in county court to have the referendum thrown off the ballot. He lost in court. Then he lost again when it came time to vote on the change. Following the election, members of the committee were charged with rewriting the municipal code. What followed were a string of confrontations with the new code. Council also backed down from a plan to review the positions of several borough directors after a public outcry. Borough officials had asked for resignation letters from several administrators in an attempt to gain leverage over them. Council and DeAngelis sparred over the applicability of provisions for a search committee—the body charged with making recommendations for appointments. Council claimed that until the administrative code was revised, references to the mayor's office essentially voided portions of the code. They didn't have to follow the portion of the code that refers to a search committee. A slot for a public safety director— who would oversee the police and fire departments—also remains unfilled. Council has also embarked on an effort to build new relationships with other government entities, getting the District Attorney's office to promise more aid from the CLEAN Team (a joint task force combining county detectives with Norristown police officers to target quality of life crimes). Council has also presided over a massive cost-cutting endeavor that has turned a projected deficit in 2004 to an almost $900,000 surplus to be used to offset another projected deficit in 2005. That cost cutting endeavor has also led to the layoff of eight borough police officers, two firefighters and several other municipal workers.

The importance of the above story cannot be overstated. Norristown was a train wreck waiting to happen, which it did. In April 2004, Norristown Borough Hall was raided by the Federal Bureau of Investigation. The home of Norristown Mayor Ted LeBlanc also was raided, along with a bar he owed on Main Street, Morely's 21st Amendment Bar. The raids were wide sweeping and successful. LeBlanc was indicted, along with borough manager Anthony Biondi, in July 2005. Other players in the pay to play scheme in Norristown also went down as a result of the raids. Norristown seemed to be down for the count.

But the raids turned out to be cathartic for Norristown. While the reputation of the town is still bruised, there have been a number of projects in recent years that point to Norristown's revitalization. Streets have been paved for the first time in more than a decade. New sidewalks have been put down in the West Marshall Street and Main Street business districts. The state Department of Environmental Protection constructed a "green" building at Main and Swede Streets for its Southeastern Pennsylvania headquarters. There are plans for an Avenue of the Arts along DeKalb Street, where new sidewalks also have been installed and new façades are going up, thanks to state grants. A deal is close on a film studio in the former Logan Square shopping center, which is now called Studio Centre.

There have been a few ups and downs during the town's journey from Norris to Norristown, but it appears as if the town is on its way up once again.

TRANSPORTATION

Like in most towns, the mode of transportation in the early years in Norristown was horse and buggy. But the Schuylkill River was seen as the best possibility for moving goods, and the first canal surveyed in the colonies in 1762 was upriver from Norristown, just below Reading, connecting the Schuylkill River to the Susquehanna River. David Rittenhouse and William Smith headed up the project and would attempt to connect the Schuylkill River to the Delaware River along a course from Norristown to Philadelphia in 1792. After many attempts and nearly fifteen miles completed, the company eventually abandoned the project. The western edge of the canal was started on the Norristown side of the Schuylkill River. Years later, in 1826, the Schuylkill Navigation Company would complete a series of locks along the river that would allow goods to be shipped inland.

Years after the first steam locomotive chugged into Norristown on August 15, 1835, the first passenger train glided into the county seat. The first trolley car ran in Norristown in 1893, even though legislation had been passed in 1866 authorizing the formation of the Norristown Passenger Railway Company, which was intended to create a horse-drawn railway.

Norristown's Halcyon Days

The trolley line was extended in 1894 to Jeffersonville in West Norriton and from Norristown into Conshohocken, eventually taking passengers all the way to Pottstown heading west and Chestnut Hill for passengers heading east. The Philadelphia & Western rail line was established in Norristown in 1912. The line crossed Main Street at Swede Street, which is depicted in the cover photo of this book. The P&W, as it was called in those days, joined the line of the Lehigh Valley Liberty Bell, which brought passengers in from Allentown. The station for both lines was located in the Rambo House Hotel. Eventually, the P&W built a new station at Main and Swede Streets. The train station has long since been abandoned, but when the Department of Environmental Protection decided to put a regional office in Norristown, it kept the façade of the old train station. Today, the Southeastern Pennsylvania Transportation Authority provides passenger rail service between Norristown and Philadelphia. The Norristown Transportation Center at Lafayette and Cherry Streets is the main hub but service also extends into Norristown at Main and Markley and onto Elm and Markley Streets.

Trains and trolleys carried Norristonians to all points east and west, north and south at the turn of the twentieth century. Accidents occurred, but none so large in scope as the Exeter train wreck. On May 12, 1899, forty people

The train depot at Main and Markley Streets was actually much larger than it is today. It is currently not much more than a shelter.

were killed, sixteen from Norristown, when the Reading Railway train was returning from the dedication of the statue of General John Frederick Hartranft in Harrisburg. The passenger train ran head-on into another train waiting for a freight train to get out of the way so it could pull off the track. The following is an account from the May 3, 1962 edition of *The Times Herald*, which carried a special section dedicated to the celebration of the sesquicentennial of Norristown:

Most of the passengers in the tragic accident were members and friends of the Montgomery Fire Company, and Company F. Sixth Regiment, Pennsylvania National Guard. The members of the Phoenixville Military Band also were in the other cars, but fortunately, no lives were lost in that group. The accident, so appalling in its suddenness, so terrible in its immediate results brought a week of funeral processions and greater desolation to Norristown than ever came to it in any time in the history of the preceding wars. The memory of the terrible occurrence remained for many years with some residents of Montgomery County. Those killed from Norristown were: John Slingluff, Chief of the Norristown Fire Department; President of the Board of Inspectors of Montgomery County Prison; President of the Montgomery National Bank and foremost in financial and other public affairs. William Stahler, a member of town council, a leading merchant and director of banks and many other public corporations. William Camm, also a member of Council, and though retired from active business, yet closely was identified with the enterprise of the borough. Col. George Schall, a good soldier and a good citizen, twice Burgess and then Postmaster of Norristown. Franklin D. Sower, a leading merchant high in business and social circles. Henry Wentz, ex-president of Town Council, President of Montgomery Hose and Steam Engine Company, director of First National Bank and other corporations. William H. Lewis, veteran of the Civil War and a merchant of integrity. Charles H. White, real estate dealer, always active in municipal matters. Capt. J. Henry Coulston and Samuel W. McCarty, veterans of Hartranft's famous regiment. John Kuntz, a representative citizen who long tenanted the Hartranft's rural domain. Henry H. Thompson, an employe of the Reading railway company, respected for his industry and admirable personal characteristics. Isaac E. Fillman, veteran of the Civil War. Joseph Taylor. Nornam Holmes, a young lad, killed by the same fatality that wounded his father. William D. Jenkins, a long time employe of Hooven's furnace.

The "One Lung Cadillac" was one of the first automobiles in Norristown. The Cloud family is believed to be the third in town to own an automobile. *Courtesy of the Cloud family ancestors.*

In 1899, the first automobile was spotted in Norristown, and by 1906 the Norristown Automobile Club was formed. Transportation in Norristown had arrived. The Cloud family of Norristown was one of the first to purchase an automobile, in 1903. Their "one-lung" Cadillac was purchased at the John Wanamaker store in Philadelphia and was believed to be the third automobile in the county seat.

Fire Companies

Soon after the borough was incorporated in 1812, a meeting was held with the intent of purchasing a fire engine. The meeting was held June 4, 1813, in Jared Brooke's tavern, and when it was over it was decided that a hand pumper, the Pat Lyon, would be purchased for $700, with the county kicking in $150 of the purchase price. The county also gave permission for the pumper to be housed in a building at the public square.

Every resident of the borough was a firefighter back then. If an alarm was sounded, all hands available were expected to grab a leather bucket, which were kept in every home, and head to the fire scene. The pumper would be dragged to the fire and residents would form lines to pass buckets of water from the nearest well to the engine. Men would crank the handles on the pump, forcing the water through a short hose with a nozzle.

Fighting fires would remain a community concern for years. However, on June 22, 1819, at a meeting once again at Brooke's tavern, the first fire company was formed in Norristown for the purpose of taking care of the fire engine. In 1827, the fire company bought a secondhand pumper and also enlarged its building to accommodate the new purchase.

These first meetings and first purchases, while recorded in the pages of the local newspapers, were not officially recorded. There are records of a company being incorporated in June 1839, when the Norristown Company was formed, headed by Benjamin F. Hancock, president, and William Slingluff, treasurer. Benjamin F. Hancock had yet to rise to fame as the father of Civil War general Winfield S. Hancock.

Norristown had its second fire company when the Good Intent Hose Company was originally formed in 1836. Both companies were around during the same time, but the Norristown Company was the first to incorporate. The Good Intent Hose Company supplied the hose to the Norristown Company, which had two engines but no extensive lines of hose. Later that same year, the Perseverance Fire Company was formed, and the Norristown Company handed over one of its engines to the newly formed company.

The Vigilant Bucket Company was formed in 1844 with the intent of taking the place of residents having to carry buckets to fires. The new company provided a horse-drawn wagon for carrying the buckets and was housed on Penn Street, just below Swede Street.

The primitive means of fighting fires was soon to come to an end, however, as Norristown had been busy laying water mains and, in 1847, put the finishing touches on a reservoir at DeKalb and Basin Streets. Fire hydrants were placed along the streets where the water mains were laid.

About a month before the town was fitted with water mains, the old fire companies came out to battle its last fire at what was described as an "old mill" at the foot of Swede Street on the banks of the river. The mill was most likely the first erected shortly after the Town of Norris was formed in 1784.

The Norristown Hose Company incorporated on February 22, 1848, and elected Jonathan R. Breitenbach, Esquire, its president. B.E. Chain was elected vice-president, while Z.T. Galt was named secretary and I.T. Moore Jr. treasurer. Just ten days later, the Montgomery Hose and Steam Fire Engine Company was formed, and in addition to its firefighting duties it also provided a community center for residents of the North End. Montgomery Hose was led by John J. Freedley, president, and B.D. Potts, secretary. Several members of Montgomery Hose were killed in the train wreck in Exeter, just outside Reading, while returning from a statue dedication in Harrisburg. The Humane Engine Company No. 1 was formed on July 27, 1852. Originally located on Airy Street, the company moved to Main and Green Streets in 1888, where it still stands today. The Fairmount Engine Company No. 2 was formed the same year as Humane. The fifth and final fire company, Hancock Fire Company, was formed on November 7, 1895, to serve the West End of town.

Hospitals

At one point, there were three public hospitals thriving in Norristown, as well as the Norristown State Hospital, which at one time in its history housed thousands of mentally afflicted patients. Norristown State Hospital, which is

The original Charity Hospital was located on Powell Street in a former schoolhouse, opening its doors in 1891. Charity Hospital was the forerunner to Montgomery Hospital, which still stands today but is moving to East Norriton.

still operating today, although with only a few hundred patients, was the first hospital built in Norristown.

In 1889, the Norristown Hospital and Dispensary was formed, but the name was changed the following year to Charity Hospital to avoid confusion with the name of the state hospital. The name was changed again in 1920 to Montgomery Hospital, which still stands today, although a merger with the Einstein Healthcare Network of Philadelphia has resulted in a future move of the hospital to East Norriton Township. The original Charity Hospital was located on Powell Street in a former schoolhouse and opened its doors in 1891. Two years later, a nursing school was established.

Sacred Heart Hospital, which is now the home of the county's human services department at DeKalb and Fornance Streets, opened for business in 1936, under the auspices of the Philadelphia Archdiocese and the Missionary Order of the Most Sacred Heart of Jesus. The hospital thrived in its early years, and plans for a new hospital were underway in 1946, eventually resulting in a new addition, the St. Joseph's Wing, being dedicated in 1948. A few years later, in 1953, fifteen additional rooms, along with a doctors'

Montgomery Hospital as seen from above in 1967.

library, were dedicated, and construction continued. In 1957, the Marian Wing was opened, and plans were underway for a nursing school. That same year, the Sacred Heart Wing was opened with thirty-eight additional beds, a chapel, a new lab and administrative offices. Three years later, ground was broken for the construction of a new convent, which was dedicated in 1961. Quick expansion and competition can be blamed for the eventual closing of Sacred Heart Hospital in May 1994.

Riverview Osteopathic Hospital opened in 1944 on Sandy Street in the East End. It had been in operation since 1917. The hospital was closed in 1972 when a new hospital, Suburban General, was built in East Norriton. Suburban General merged with Mercy Health Systems and is now called Mercy Suburban.

Norristown State Hospital has been shrinking in patient size for the past several decades, mostly due to the advent of psychiatric drugs and a new way of thinking that encourages community integration of the mentally ill. There are dozens of buildings on the site, which is on the West End of town

Norristown State Hospital has been shrinking in patient size for the past several decades, mostly due to the advent of psychiatric drugs and a new way of thinking that encourages community integration of the mentally ill. There are dozens of buildings on the site that have fallen into disrepair. *Courtesy of the author.*

and actually spreads into West Norriton Township. Plans are underway for the demolition of some of the buildings, and a new state police dispatch center was built on the campus a few years ago.

HISTORIC BUILDINGS

Unfortunately, many of Norristown's historic buildings have been demolished over the years. The architectural splendor that once dominated the county seat can still be found, but unfortunately, most of it is in some form of disrepair.

The Gresh Mansion, which still stands today, has been used as a storage facility for the past two decades. The mansion has not been used as a private residence for years. There are many other once private mansions that have been converted either to commercial or multifamily along West Main Street. This area once was the place to live in Norristown, especially after the construction in the 1870s of the bridge spanning Stony Creek made it easily accessible.

Heading north on DeKalb Street just past Brown Street, both sides of the road are filled with beautiful homes. These are the homes of judges, developers and obviously wealthy people who take pride in their homes.

The predominant dwelling in Norristown is the row home, but they're not to be quickly driven by. Many of the homes have ornate brickwork adorning their façades. Twin homes also dominate many of the streets in Norristown.

A quick scan of a Sanborn Map of Norristown from October 1896 shows the "Biggest Borough in the World" well on its way to becoming so. Stony Creek is spanned at Main Street and West Marshall Street, aiding the growth of the West End at that early time in the borough's history. However, heading north on Markley Street, a traveler would only have gotten as far as Airy Street. The Dannehower Bridge was yet to be built, and the land north of Airy is described as "vacant and unimproved."

The map lists the population of Norristown at twenty-two thousand in 1896 and describes the public water system as a gravity system of waterworks with a ten-million-gallon reservoir. It was located two miles north of the courthouse at an elevation of two hundred feet above the Schuylkill River. Water was moved through a twenty-four-inch main by a Worthington pump. Norristown's fire department at the time was all volunteer and was aided by a Gamewell Fire Alarm System with sixteen boxes. There were four

The Gresh Mansion, once the home of W.K. Gresh, owner of one of three cigar factories in Norristown, is used for storage these days.

first-class steam fire engines, four hose carts, two hose wagons, four hose carriages, three supply wagons, one hook and ladder truck, two chemical engines and six thousand feet of two-and-a-half-inch standard hose "in good condition."

The Sanborn-Perris Map Co. Limited labeled the map an "insurance map" and listed all of the commercial properties in the heart of the town. Only sixteen years away from its centennial celebration, Norristown was thriving.

There were seventeen hotels in Norristown at the time, including the Yearle's and the Exchange, along with the Hotel Beldow, Hotel Finley, Hotel Germania and Hotel Montgomery. There were sixteen mills, including the C.G. Morgan Flour Mill and the Norristown Carpet Mill. There also were sixteen churches in Norristown at the turn of the century. St. Patrick was the first Catholic church in town. Ebenezer already was established as well as Mount Zion AME, All Saints and Central Presbyterian. There were three cigar manufacturing plants, and oddly enough, with all of this activity only two stores were listed on the map. There were five public schools in town,

The YMCA on Airy Street as it appeared in 1981. The Norristown YMCA was organized September 11, 1885.

The YWCA as it appeared in 1989.

most of which were named after the streets on which they were located. Naming a school after a person wouldn't become popular for many years to come. Two breweries, Scheidt's and Cox, were operating, and Norristown even had an opera house.

Manufacturing dominated in those days. More than forty plants were in operation in 1896.

Norristown once was home to a YMCA (located on Airy Street between DeKalb and Swede Streets, built in 1927) and a YWCA, but as with most cities of this size, the population just hasn't been able to support either of the Christian organizations. Both buildings have been razed. The loss of both the YMCA and the YWCA left a void that is being filled only by the George Washington Carver Community Center. The fledgling Norristown Police Athletic League (PAL) operated without a home for many years until a group of concerned citizens and police officers got together to find a home for the athletic organization that has evolved into a place for children to go for a variety of activities. The Norristown PAL is now located in the former Stewart Armory on Harding Boulevard.

Norristown's Halcyon Days

The Stewart Armory on Harding Boulevard is now the home of the Norristown Police Athletic League.

One of Norristown's most famous buildings was the once grand Valley Forge Hotel, which was built in 1925 at the pinnacle of Norristown's halcyon days. The Valley Forge Hotel was the place to be seen back in the day. Senator John F. Kennedy stopped at the Valley Forge Hotel on his way to make a speech at Roosevelt Field. A reporter for the *Norristown Times Herald* was waiting to interview Kennedy when he heard him complaining about an editorial in that day's edition of the paper. Kennedy was said to have voiced his displeasure, in a rather upset and loud voice, just moments before the reporter was led into the room.

The Bell Telephone building on DeKalb Street, between Main and Airy Streets, was once a private home. The telephone company later built a substantial structure at Penn and Cherry Streets, which also still stands today. Both buildings have been renovated and are awaiting new tenants.

On Airy Street, between DeKalb and Swede Streets, was and still is the post office, which was built in 1934. At that time, the Reformed Church of the Ascension was located next door, but it was soon razed to make way for the expansion of the county courthouse. The old post office was at Main and Barbadoes Streets.

The Rambo House sat at the corner of Swede and Airy Streets next to the First Baptist Church.

Complementing all of the historic buildings in Norristown were, and still remain, some beautiful residences, especially along the northern portion of DeKalb Street. Many of the private residences that once dominated West Main Street have been converted into businesses or torn down.

Still one of the most visible buildings in Norristown, the county courthouse, as it stands today, is much larger than the original version, which was completed in 1854. The original courthouse, which was built immediately following the forming of the county, was located on the same tract of land. Four years went into the building of the present-day county courthouse, with work beginning in 1851 after the selection of the architect, Napoleon Eugene Henry Charles LeBrun of Philadelphia. LeBrun was the architect behind the Academy of Music in Philadelphia as well as the Cathedral of Saints Peter and Paul. Instead of having the courthouse face the public square, LeBrun situated his plans to have the building face Swede Street. After much public outrage, the plans were eventually accepted and work began. The imposing structure is built of marble taken from Montgomery County quarries, most in Upper Merion, and garnered the nickname the "marble palace" because of its outrageous $150,000 price tag. A steeple once adorned the top of the courthouse, which is now recognizable for its copper dome.

During the maneuvering to make room for the new courthouse, a move was afoot to have the county seat relocated to Center Square in Whitpain Township. The fight made its way all the way to the state legislature but eventually was defeated.

Once the new courthouse was built, the old courthouse was demolished. A marble date stone with the inscription "Montgomery County 1791" was saved, however, and placed in a retaining wall along Swede Street.

Additions to the original structure have been made over the course of the past century, but the original six massive columns remain untouched. There are several significant markers on the grounds of the courthouse, including an obelisk in honor of David Rittenhouse, which is inscribed, "David Rittenhouse, Eminent Astronomer and Mathematician, Born April 8 1732, Died June 26, 1796." Another marker simply states, "This is the site of the first Montgomery County Prison erected 1786." That marker is in the far northwest corner of the grounds.

While not historic in age, the home of the Historical Society of Montgomery County deserves a mention here. Norristown has been blessed to have two institutions dedicated to preserving its history. *The Times Herald* has been around longer than the municipality itself and has recorded its history every step of the way. By its side, at least for the past 128 years, has been the Historical Society of Montgomery County, whose home can be found on DeKalb Street in the North End of town. To this day, *The Times Herald* still provides microfilm copies of every edition of the paper to the society.

A rather large group gathered at the courthouse in 1881 to establish the historical society, and their names will be remembered by history buffs throughout the county. The original twenty-three members included two Corsons, two Beans and an Iredell. General William J. Bolton also was a founding member, along with Nathaniel Jacoby. Other later members included Joseph K. Gotwals and Joseph Fornance. Many of the names above can be seen on street signs, office buildings, schoolhouses and other places of importance throughout Norristown.

The society soon outgrew its place at the courthouse, as had Norristown's government, which made its home at 18 East Penn Street. The society purchased the building in 1896, when a Norristown borough hall was built at Airy and DeKalb Streets. Some thirty years later, the society was outgrowing its first home, and Ralph Beaver Strassburger, owner of the *Norristown Times Herald* at the time, began a campaign to raise the money necessary to find a new home for the historical society. However, it wasn't until 1954 that the society would finally settle into its new home on DeKalb Street, where the massive collection still resides today.

While many of the buildings that housed turn-of-the-century businesses, including the Montgomery Bank building on Main Street, still stand as a testament to the town's industrious past, the homes in Norristown are just as distinct for their architectural style. Doug Seiler, a local architect, describes Norristown as a Victorian town. "It's really a nineteenth-century town. The basic brick buildings are called Greek Revival. The whole West End didn't develop until the Main Street bridge was built [over Stony Creek near Markley Street]. Over a few decades the whole West End was developed."

Once the bridge was in place, the West End began to flourish. While mostly residential, there were several mills and manufacturing plants, and the still standing cigar factory, which has been converted into loft apartments, taking up residence as well.

The West End established its own business district early on, with shops lining both sides of West Marshall Street from Corson Street to Kohn Street. Only in later years have businesses set up shop on West Main Street. Residents of the West End even had their very own movie theatre, the West Mar, which still stands today, with a shoe store now taking up residence. Most of the industry in the West End was concentrated along Stony Creek and the Schuylkill River, with the Tyson Shirt Factory setting up shop adjacent to the W.K. Gresh Cigar Factory on Corson Street, both of which used Stony Creek to their advantage. The West End also was home to the Ballard Knitting Mill on West Washington Street, as well as the Wilcombe Machine Co. and the Lee Harris Manufacturing Co.

West Main Street, with its mixture of row homes, semidetached homes and single-family homes, contains an eclectic mix of architectural styles. Several of the single-family homes, many of which have since been converted into apartment buildings, have turrets and watchtowers. The architectural style is predominantly Victorian. The West End flourished almost as a town of its own. Schools and churches were built to accommodate the local residents. In 1871, a school was built at Chain and Airy Streets, and the John F. Hartranft school took its place in 1894. Churches began to spring up in quick succession. Haws Avenue Methodist Church was established in 1875 and Calvary Baptist, at Haws Avenue and West Marshall Street, was established in 1887.

"There's only one or two buildings that are colonial," Seiler continued. "The British burned everything." History has it that during the Revolutionary War, British general William Howe came through Norristown, burning buildings along the way, before moving on to Germantown to rest his troops before his triumphant entrance into Philadelphia. The most logical place of encampment would have been between DeKalb and Swede Streets, perhaps where the town square would soon be established once America had gained its independence.

An account in the local paper described Howe's occupation of Norristown in monetary terms: "While in this vicinity in September, 1777, the British burned considerable property, among which was the powder mill. Damages for the property destroyed were allowed by the government after the war as follows: To John Bull, 2,080 pounds; to the University of Pennsylvania, 1,000 pounds; to Hannah Thompson, 807 pounds; to William Dewees, 329 pounds." John Bull's mill was located at the foot of Swede Street near the Schuylkill River.

Seiler continued,

Main Street is pretty much Victorian. It continued to get torn down and rebuilt until the early twentieth century. The Norris Theatre, the DEP building, which is the old P&W, they're examples of Art Deco. The P&W was an elevated train. There was a streetcar that went up DeKalb.

The lawyers would take the streetcar up DeKalb and then take the train back. It must have been a pretty nice life.

One of the oldest buildings on Main Street is the former Montgomery Bank. It has some great history to it. That is pure Greek Revival. There are Montgomery County Civil War dollars with that bank on it. The building immediately to the left of it, that was the bank owner's house.

There are several other historic buildings still standing on Main Street today, including the Odd Fellows building and the Masonic lodge, which originally was the home of James Hooven, president of the former First National Bank of Norristown, which later merged with Montgomery Trust. The Rambo & Regar building still stands today on the east end of Main Street and has undergone renovations. Many of today's old-timers will remember the Conte Luna macaroni factory, also on the east end of Main Street, which also is being renovated into office space.

The real wealth that was happening, the owners of the mills built those mansions along West Main Street. All that gingerbread stuff falls under Victorian. I have noticed, and the West End has it, sort of a Norristown vernacular. They have a particular way the bricks are corbelled. There's a particular sort of double window with brackets at the gabled end that I've only seen in Norristown. It could have been other places, I've seen a couple in Bridgeport, but they're all over Norristown.

Seiler had to weigh in on fellow architect Napoleon Lebrun's Norristown work, the Montgomery County Courthouse:

The courthouse had a steeple on it. Napoleon LeBrun was a Catholic. The steeple was a statement of Catholic pride. I thought it was interesting that he put a symbol of the Catholic Church on a Greek Revival building. In LeBrun's case, I think he was making a statement. LeBrun won the right to build the courthouse and the prison in a national contest. He won it over Thomas Walter.

Walter built the Presbyterian church, which had a dome that is the precursor to the capital dome that Walter later built.

Seiler said that the most historically significant building depends on what makes a building significant: "The building I can think of that has something to do with a person, which would be the Thaddeus Lowe House. The other one that strikes me is First Presbyterian church across from us [Airy and

DeKalb Streets]. It's so significant because it can be seen from miles around, and you can't ignore the courthouse because of its significance."

Seiler is a principal in the Seiler Drury Architecture firm, located in the former Yost Interiors furniture store, which has quite a history of its own.

> *The windows in this building were done by Edwin Braumbaugh. Yost had him put them in when he made it a department store. It's been a furniture store in our era, but it was a department store at one point and then it shrunk into the furniture store. Daniel Yost remembers that every day when he was a kid he would take the ladder up to the widow's watch and raise the flag. This building is known as the Jamison House.*

Jamison House was built in 1850 by the son of the owner of Jamison Mills, William Jamison, and is considered a Greek Revival–style home.

"What's historic about Norristown architecturally is the Norristown State Hospital," Seiler continued. "It was built by the Wilson brothers. They did the whole campus. It's an extraordinary collection. That's what you call high Victorian."

Churches

Churches have been a part of Norristown since its earliest days. From the first Quaker settlers, immigrants who eventually would call Norristown home would also bring their religion with them.

The first organized church in Norristown is believed to be St. John's Episcopal Church, which is still thriving at its original location on Airy Street just across from the county courthouse. St. John's was formed the same year Norristown was incorporated, in 1812. The Reverend Jehu Curtis Clay was the first clergyman assigned to St. John's, in 1814, when the original church was completed. There have been additions to the church over the years, but the original house of worship is still an inspiring structure. Behind the church is a cemetery that is adjacent to the back walls of the old county prison. A few years after St. John's was established, members of the Lower Providence Presbyterian Church moved into town and in 1819 formed the First Presbyterian Church, which is also still standing today at DeKalb and Airy Streets. The spire of the church can be seen for miles around. A closer examination of the spire reveals a tilt

The First Presbyterian Church on Airy Street is recognizable by its spire, which has begun to tilt. *Courtesy of the author.*

toward the north that has been some cause for concern over the years, but measures have been taken to make sure it is secure.

The First Baptist Church was established at Airy and Swede Streets but later moved to its current home on Burnside Avenue in West Norriton Township. While it was thriving in Norristown, the First Baptist Church became a stop on the Underground Railroad and also hosted some of this nation's most famous abolitionists. There will be more on First Baptist later in this book. The Second Baptist Church was located on Marshall Street at Haws Avenue and had a Sunday school facing Haws Avenue as well.

Norristown is home to more than eighty churches today, many of which formed in the early days of the town. Mount Zion AME Church on Willow Street was the first formed for the African American population in Norristown. Bethany Evangelical United Brethren Church, at Marshall and Swede Streets, was originally established on Cherry Street between Marshall and Airy Streets. Grace Evangelical Lutheran was located on George Street at Blackberry Alley at the turn of the nineteenth century. Trinity Reformed Lutheran was at Marshall and Cherry Streets.

Marshall Street is home to a host of churches. The Haws Avenue Methodist Congregation was formed in 1875. The church was under construction in 1896 and still stands today. Calvary Baptist can be found at the same intersection.

The first Catholic church in the county, St. Patrick Roman Catholic Church, on Washington Street between Barbadoes and Cherry Streets, was dedicated in 1839 by Bishop Kenrick and eventually moved to its new home on DeKalb Street, where the faithful still gather. St. Patrick was and still is home to the descendants of the Irish immigrants who helped establish Norristown as an industrial center. St. Patrick Parish was established in 1835, celebrating 150 years in 1985. The church has opened its doors to the new influx of Mexican immigrants who now call Norristown home. Sunday services often include more than two hundred people. The Hispanic population that started the Sunday trend at St. Patrick was of Puerto Rican descent.

Although Norristown's namesake, Isaac Norris, was a devout Quaker, the first Friends meetinghouse was not established until 1862 at Swede and Jacoby Streets; it still stands today.

Small in numbers, but nonetheless dedicated, a Jewish community group founded the Tiferes Israel Synagogue in 1901 at the site of the former

Trinity Reformed Church on Marshall Street. A Jewish Community Center was established in 1936 at Brown and Powell Streets.

Large in numbers, perhaps the largest of all the congregations in Norristown, is that of Holy Saviour Roman Catholic Church on Main Street in the east end of town, attended faithfully to this day by a large contingent of members of Italian descent. Parishioners sent their children to Holy Saviour School at Airy and Walnut Streets, formerly the Welsh School, for many years until the school was closed after combining with Our Lady of Victory in East Norriton Township. The church, along with the town of Norristown, has a "sister" in Montella, Italy, where a large number of Italian immigrants began their migration to the United States. Norristown and Montella are linked through the international Sister Cities program, which has been in existence since 1991. To this day, the Montellesi keep the connection with their homeland. As far as the Italian immigrants are concerned, Norristown's sister city just as easily could have been Sciacca, a small town in Sicily, that many of Norristown's Italian families once called home.

Schools

The first public school in Norristown, the Norristown Public School House, was built on a tract of land just east of the public square, which had been sold to the borough by the University of Pennsylvania to be held "in trust for the use of a public school to be established and maintained in Norristown forever." Payment for the land was to be an acorn a year, if demanded. According to a list of buildings compiled by *Norristown Gazette* publisher David Sower in 1800, the school was apparently built in the northeast corner of the land near Penn Street.

Norristown Academy succeeded in its location at Airy and DeKalb Streets. Built in 1805, for many years it was the only school in town. It was eventually torn down in 1829 to make way for the extension of DeKalb Street, which stopped at Airy Street at the turn of the nineteenth century. The oldest schoolhouse still standing in Norristown is at Airy and Cherry Streets and is the home of the Montgomery Bar Association.

The public school system as we know it today began in 1834 through a state law. Although there are indications that Norristown was home to "public" schools before that time, tuition was required to attend some of the local schools.

A grand structure located at DeKalb and Oak Streets was the home of Norristown High School. It was built in 1880 and dedicated on August 19 of that year. The dedication was reported in the press and was described in a brief article:

The new school building on DeKalb St., above Oak, was formally dedicated on Saturday afternoon to the purpose for which it was erected, in the presence of several hundred ladies, gentlemen and children interested in the work of education.

Early in the afternoon, the doors of the structure were thrown open and an opportunity was given to all who desired it, to inspect the new building.

About 2:45 o'clock when Prof. J.K. Gotwals, Superintendent of Public Schools, called the meeting to order, the space on the rear of the teacher's desk was taken by the School Board of Norristown, who occupied chairs, as did Dr. J.P. Wickersham, Superintendent of Public Instruction in Pennsylvania.

Others taking seats were: Rev. Isaac Gibson, Rector of St. John's P.E. Church; Theo W. Bean and others. While on the platform to the right of them sat Prof. R.F. Hoffecker, Superintendent of Public Schools in Montgomery County; Prof. A.D. Eisenhower, Principal of the Norristown High School; and the following ex-members of the Norristown High School; Adam Slemmer, Isaac H. Miller, Nathaniel Jacoby, A.H. Baker and Charles Ramsey.

The high school was moved fifty-eight years later when a new high school was built at Markley Street and Coolidge Boulevard. The new Norristown Senior High School was dedicated on June 14, 1938, and was later renamed after the former principal of Norristown High School, A.D. Eisenhower. Norristown Area High School, which is actually in West Norriton Township, was built in 1972 and A.D. Eisenhower became a middle school. There have been several elementary schools throughout the years in the district, which comprises Norristown, East Norriton and West Norriton. Currently, there are six elementary schools, three middle schools and the high school. The Roosevelt School, located on Markley Street, is currently used as an alternative school; however, the football field is still used by the high school. Talks are underway concerning the construction of a new football stadium and track at the high school in West Norriton.

Should any parent reading this tend to lapse into a nostalgic longing for the more wholesome times of their school days, a reprinting of a portion of a 1941 column from *The Times Herald* reveals that parents of every generation thought that there was always something nefarious taking place in the schools:

Of course, the schools of the 1870's were far different from those of today. There were no sports nor athletics, except what the students achieved through their own inventiveness on the school grounds. No school societies existed and no school publications. Students of today would wonder what was the use of going to school in the 1870's.

But even in the 1870's some innovations were introduced in the Norristown schools that failed to meet general approval. Thus, following the commencement of 1874, a letter, signed, "An Old-Fashioned Thinker," appeared in the Herald saying:

"From all quarters I hear unqualified approval of the closing exercises of the Oak Street School, but every sensible person present was struck with the ridiculous display of dress on this occasion. When we think that these elaborately flounced young ladies, with hair crimped and powdered, with expensive sashes, double buttoned kid gloves and slippers, are simply school girls, we are sure something must be radically wrong with the parents, we care not what their worldly circumstances may be, who will allow such unnecessary display."

Unfortunately, "elaborately flounced" was not expanded upon.

Bishop Kenrick Catholic High School became Norristown's second Catholic high school when it opened its doors to 664 students on February 6, 1956, succeeding St. Patrick Catholic High School, which held its first graduation in 1945 and its last in 1955. By 1962, enrollment at the high school had grown to 1,763. Bishop Kenrick later merged with Conshohocken's Archbishop Kennedy Catholic High School and became Kennedy Kenrick Catholic High School, remaining in Norristown at its current location on Johnson Highway at Arch Street. However, low enrollment during the past several years has led the Archdiocese of Philadelphia to purchase land in Upper Providence Township for a new high school, merging Kennedy Kenrick with St. Pius X in Pottstown. The new school, which is expected to open for the 2010–11 school year, will be called John Paul II.

PART II

The Names
of Norristown

What's in a name? A lot, if you're from Norristown. From the birth of the biggest borough in the world, Norristown has been home to an impressive number of famous characters, especially for a town that even during its halcyon days boasted a population that never reached the forty thousand mark.

From the town's namesake, Isaac Norris, to baseball's most prolific home run hitting catcher, Mike Piazza, high achievers have either been born and raised here or migrated to Norristown for one reason or another. But as you'll find out later in the book, nicknames were a way of life during the early to middle portion of the twentieth century. From Mungo to Muffy and from Jinks to Popeye, the cast of characters playing on the ball fields and basketball courts were as colorful as their nicknames.

CIVIL WAR GENERALS

While Norristown is surrounded by battlegrounds of the Revolutionary War and was once dubbed the "Gateway to Valley Forge," where General George Washington rested his soldiers during the winter of 1777, the town is perhaps best known for the number of Civil War generals who called Norristown home. Five Civil War generals, all of whom fought for the North, are buried in Montgomery Cemetery, which lies on the western edge of town. Montgomery Cemetery was established in 1847 as one of the first public cemeteries on the East Coast. The Civil War generals mentioned here are all buried in the Grand Army of the Republic plot.

General Winfield S. Hancock, Norristown's most famous son of the Civil War era, was born in Montgomery Township, along with his twin brother, Hilary, on February 14, 1824. However, before the twins would reach the age of five, the Hancock family moved to a little stone house at the corner of Selma and Washington Streets in Norristown. Winfield's father, Benjamin F. Hancock, an attorney, would later build a house on Swede Street near Middleton Alley. Winfield's father was a teacher and later became an attorney, setting up practice on Swede Street. He named his son after Winfield Scott, a United States Army general.

At the tender age of fifteen, Winfield S. Hancock was selected to attend West Point, where his life as a soldier began. Hancock's first active duty was in the Mexican War of 1846, where he served with honor. When the Civil War began in 1861, he was appointed brigadier and led a troop of volunteers in the Army of the Potomac. Hancock eventually attained the rank of major general and distinguished himself at the Battle of Gettysburg and during the Peninsula Campaign, where he earned the nickname "Hancock the Superb." A wound suffered at the Battle of Gettysburg, and other previous wounds, would eventually end his military career, but not before he returned to battle with Ulysses S. Grant. After recuperating at his home in Norristown, Hancock joined Grant for the Battle of Spotsylvania in Virginia, which eventually made it possible for the Union army to reach Richmond, where Robert E. Lee surrendered the Army of Northern Virginia to Grant.

The W.S. Hancock Society of Norristown is active in reenactments, or living history programs, especially at Gettysburg and Montgomery Cemetery. Karin Stocking founded the W.S. Hancock Society, along with her father, Paul Koons. She remarked:

We have very few folks that have hailed from Norristown that have gone on to hit the national scene. Winfield Hancock not only hit the national scene but was actually known worldwide. He was well known, well liked and he was a true person. He was unpretentious. He didn't go out and blow his own horn like many of the other generals did. That's probably the reason he fell into obscurity. When the movie came out, he started getting attention again. It was about that time that we started the preservation of his mausoleum.

Stocking said that they started the society in the summer of 1994 to bring Hancock's name back into the American consciousness.

"People still remember Winfield Scott, and of course Winfield Scott Hancock was named after him, but he's often confused for him," Stocking said.

"Hancock was known as the hero of Gettysburg and was asked to come to Washington when Lincoln was assassinated to take control from a military perspective. When he ran for president in 1880, he swept the South, although he didn't take Pennsylvania. He was a Democrat, which in his day espoused the same ideology as a very conservative Republican of today. He was narrowly defeated in the presidential election by James A. Garfield, who was assassinated just four months after taking office. Hancock put himself on the line for what he thought was right. That's one of the things that endears him to me."

Every year at the cemetery, the society holds a Memorial Day tribute to Hancock and the other generals buried there, as well as for the everyday soldiers buried at Montgomery Cemetery. Stocking commented:

> I think since they were all from the same area, they all agreed that it was important that they get involved in the dispute between the North and South, and they felt it was important to protect their state since the Federal government wasn't as strong back then. There was a great sense of local pride that took them into battle.
>
> It is a public cemetery, so you didn't have to belong to a church to be buried at the cemetery. You can go to many cemeteries and find veterans buried throughout the county.
>
> Hancock was just one of those people who, at a very young age, had a predisposition for the military. His mother's father was a Revolutionary War Patriot.

The W.S. Hancock Society also holds walking tours at Montgomery Cemetery every year around Halloween. Legend has it that a witch and all her belongings, furniture included, were buried under a huge mound of dirt in the cemetery. There also is the story of "Headless Hunsicker," a veteran of the Civil War who was buried in an underground vault. Hunsicker received the infamous moniker when vandals broke into the vault and stole his skull, according to Stocking, who was quoted for a story in 2003 just before one of the walking tours.

John F. Hartranft was born on December 16, 1830, in Fagleysville, New Hanover Township, in western Montgomery County. Hartranft's early life was not as militarily motivated as Hancock's, as he went to Union College in New York, where he majored in engineering. After

John F. Hartranft settled in Norristown and became a deputy sheriff before his stellar military career in the Civil War, where he attained the rank of general. *Courtesy of the author.*

college, he settled in Norristown and became a deputy sheriff; later, he was admitted to the bar association. He also was a member of the Norristown Fire Company and a Freemason.

Hartranft's military career began when he was appointed colonel of the First Regiment of the Montgomery County Militia. When the Civil War erupted, the First Regiment was folded into the Fourth Pennsylvania Volunteer Infantry. When that assignment was over, Hartranft returned home and formed the Fifty-first Regiment of Infantry, dubbed "Norristown's own." The Fifty-first Regiment fought alongside Grant at Vicksburg and down through Virginia to Richmond, where Lee surrendered at Appomattox Court House. Hartranft attained the rank of major general after defeating Lee's army at the Battle of Fort Stedman. After the war, Hartranft was elected governor of Pennsylvania, serving two terms, and later became postmaster in Philadelphia.

Hartranft, along with Hancock, served at the trial of those accused in the assassination of President Lincoln. Both were reluctant to carry out the executions, especially that of Mary Surratt, the first female executed by the United States government.

Samuel K. Zook was actually of Amish descent, which one would deduce would leave him out of military service. That was not to be the case. Zook, who was born in Chester County on March 27, 1821, was influenced early in life by military matters. The Zook family moved to what is now Valley Forge National Historical Park when he was young, obtaining the house that once served as a commissary for General Washington.

The young Zook joined the 100th Regiment of the Militia but received no pay for his service, and two years later he moved to New York, where he was supervisor in charge of the installation of telegraph lines for the New York and Washington Telegraph Company. While in New York, he was appointed major of the 6th Regiment of New York Volunteers. The regiment, similar to Hartranft's 4th Pennsylvania, was only a three-month assignment, after which Zook returned to New York, formed the 57th New York Volunteers and quickly returned to the fighting. By November 1862, Zook had attained the rank of brigadier general and took command of the 2nd Corps in the Army of the Potomac. Zook was killed at the Battle of Gettysburg. His body was returned to Norristown, where he was interred at Montgomery Cemetery.

Adam J. Slemmer was born on January 24, 1828, in Frederick Township, Montgomery County. Shortly after his birth, his family moved to Norristown. Like Hancock, Slemmer was selected to attend West Point.

He was commissioned a second lieutenant but came out of the academy too late for the Mexican War of 1846. He was stationed in California and Florida and returned to West Point to teach math and English. Slemmer made a military name for himself when he was returned to Florida for an assignment. The young lieutenant was placed in command of the forts of Pensacola Bay. Slemmer and a handful of soldiers were attacked at Fort Pickens by Confederates but repelled every attempt to take the stronghold. For his bravery and obvious military guile in being able to hold the fort with such a small contingent, Slemmer was promoted to major of the Sixteenth Regiment. Slemmer served in West Virginia and Tennessee, where he was wounded at the Battle of Murfreesboro. Slemmer was then appointed brigadier general for his bravery in battle and was soon withdrawn from the field. A later assignment, after the war, found him in Fort Laramie, Wyoming, where he died suddenly.

William J. Bolton, the only true Norristonian, was born on October 22, 1833, in the county seat. His early life consisted of apprenticeships as a machinist and an engineer. He was an active Democrat, but when the Republican call to arms came in 1861, he was ready to serve. With a little military experience serving in Hartranft's militia, Bolton was assigned once again to Hartranft and his Fourth Pennsylvania Volunteer Infantry. Bolton quickly rose to the rank of captain in the infantry's brief three-month deployment. Bolton returned to Norristown with Hartranft after the short stint and helped with the formation of the Fifty-first Regiment. He was wounded at Antietam and returned home to recuperate. When he returned to the war, he was commissioned a major and soon after attained the rank of colonel, fighting with Grant at Vicksburg. He was in command of the Fifty-first Regiment at Petersburg, where he was wounded once again. Just four days after Lee surrendered, Bolton attained the rank of brigadier general.

While not a general or a Norristonian, Thaddeus Lowe, the famed inventor, did call Norristown home for a few years, during which time he produced some of his most successful inventions, including an ice-making machine that revolutionized the shipping industry. Lowe, whose Norristown home has recently been restored, is mentioned in this section of the book because of his work with the Union army, specifically under General Winfield Scott (namesake of Norristown's general Winfield Scott Hancock), who oversaw the formation of Lowe's balloon corps. Lowe was convinced that he could use hot air balloons to spy on the Confederate army and was somewhat successful in the

Thaddeus Lowe, the famed inventor, did call Norristown home for a few years, during which time he produced some of his most successful inventions, including an ice-making machine that revolutionized the shipping industry. *Courtesy of the author.*

early part of the war, including during the Battles of Sharpsburg and Fredericksburg. However, after a dispute with Congress over the effectiveness of the corps, Lowe resigned.

It also should be noted here that hundreds upon thousands of black soldiers gave their lives in the Civil War. The graves of more than thirty can be found in Treemont Cemetery in Norristown.

Sports Figures

Norristown has produced a number of sports figures over the years. The early days of sports can be traced through predecessors of *The Times Herald*, where stories of the first football game of Norristown High School are recalled. Lorin Rawson is credited with forming the first football team in 1892. The team played just one game that year, defeating the YMCA team 14–4 at Oak View Park on Thanksgiving Day. Roosevelt Field was opened a few years later, in 1909.

Baseball was probably the first organized sport to be played in Norristown. It was introduced in 1859 by John Roberts, according to *Montgomery County: The Second Hundred Years*. It wasn't but a few years later, after the Civil War, that clubs began springing up all over town. Just before the turn of the century, there was a club for nearly every sport imaginable, and leagues were formed soon after so that teams could compete.

Present-day Roosevelt Field was the original home of the Stockade, which was a baseball field. Once the school district bought the field, concrete stands were built and it was renamed Roosevelt Field.

Perhaps Norristown's most famous football son, Steve Bono, played at Norristown Area High School in the late 1970s. He played his collegiate career at UCLA and was drafted by the Minnesota Vikings in 1985. Bono's solid career was capped by a stellar year in 1995, when he led the Kansas City Chiefs to a 13–3 record and was selected to play in the Pro Bowl. John Pergine is another standout athlete born in Norristown. Pergine went on to play at the University of Notre Dame and then to the NFL to play for the Los Angeles Rams and the Washington Redskins. Emile Boures, while not a Norristown native, played football at Bishop Kenrick in the borough and went on to the University of Pittsburgh and then to the Pittsburgh Steelers where he played for four years.

The Names of Norristown

Baseball Greats

Baseball has a long tradition in Norristown, beginning in the early 1900s with Roy Thomas, who went on to play for the Philadelphia Phillies. Thomas was one of the most prolific lead-off hitters in Phillies history, stealing on average twenty bases a season in an eleven-year career. He led the league in batting three times and in runs scored eight times. Few people may know that the Norristown native is responsible for changing the game. Thomas could foul off dozens of balls with each at-bat. Eventually, the foul strike rule was devised to keep a batter from staying at the plate for lengthy periods, sometimes forcing a pitcher out of the game in the first inning. The foul strike rule declared that the first two foul balls would be considered strikes, forcing batters, specifically Thomas, to be much more judicious with their swings.

Norristown also boasts a couple other famous sons in the baseball world. Tom Lasorda's Major League career as a player was short-lived, but he stood at the helm of the Los Angeles Dodgers for twenty years, winning two World Series. He was named manager of the year two times, but perhaps his most rewarding accomplishment was coaching Team USA to Olympic gold in the 2000 games in Sydney, Australia.

While it has been rumored over the years that Tommy Lasorda is Mike Piazza's uncle or godfather, the truth is that Tommy Lasorda is a good friend of Vince Piazza, Mike's father, and is godfather to Mike's brother Tom. "In the Italian custom, if you're actually godfather to one, you're godfather to them all," Lasorda said of his connection to the Piazza family. When asked what it meant to him to be from Norristown, Lasorda said:

> *No matter where I've gone to, I've never forgotten where I grew up. Norristown to me was golden. Norristown, to me, will always be my love. Even though I moved to California, Norristown has always been in my heart.*
>
> *I think of my father, who worked so hard to take care of us. There are five of us, Eddie, Harry, Morris and Joey and me. We're all still alive.*

Smokey wasn't the only Lasorda with a nickname growing up—Tommy proudly donned the moniker "Mungo." "Van Lingo Mungo was a right-hand pitcher for the Brooklyn Dodgers," said Lasorda. "I took his name because I liked him. I finally met him. I shook hands with him and told him how I adopted his name. He couldn't believe it."

Lasorda, who was born on September 22, 1927, grew up on Walnut Street, just across from the Holy Saviour School. He went to Holy Saviour and then on to Rittenhouse Junior High. After that he went to Norristown High, which is now A.D. Eisenhower Middle School.

"Growing up in Norristown at Christmastime was incredible," he said. "The people were always there for everyone. I always looked at Main Street as a beautiful street. It's just not the same anymore."

Lasorda grew up with Josh Culbreath and Al Cantello, two superstars in their own right. "Josh used to eat at our house," Lasorda said. "Al Cantello used to have me down to speak. We have maintained the relationships over the years. The good friends that I developed growing up stand out very much."

But it's baseball that Lasorda remembers most.

> *I remember those days because baseball stopped me from getting into trouble. Times were tough back then, and kids were getting into trouble. We played at Elmwood Park. I remember the day we brought the Connie Mack Allstars in to play and I pitched against them. It was a big game. In order to bring that team into Norristown, we had to pay them $100 to come in. paid. Our team was composed of the high schools in the area. It was a team from Philadelphia. Connie Mack had composed his team of all the outstanding players in the Philadelphia area. That's why I remember the game so well.*
>
> *After beating them, I went down to try out for their team in Baltimore. Bobby Shantz and I made the team. We played against men. We were fifteen- and sixteen-year-old kids. That's where Jocko Collins discovered me and he signed me for $100 month. He signed three guys from that area that all managed in the Major League. It was all because of that game . It turned out to be the steppingstone for me. A lot of people came out to see the game. I couldn't sleep the night before knowing I was going to pitch that game.*

Tommy Lasorda's pride for his hometown caused him to have to do some explaining after an appearance on the short-lived *Hee Haw* country-themed comedy show: "You would get into the cornfield and you would raise up and say I'm from wherever, population forty thousand. I didn't do that. I stood up and said, 'My hometown, Norristown, is the garden spot of the United States.' The guy said, 'You weren't supposed to say all of that.' I said, 'That's

Tommy Lasorda (right) was born and raised in Norristown and went on to Major League baseball fame, winning two World Series while coaching the Los Angeles Dodgers and taking the U.S. Olympic team to the gold medal in the 2000 games in Sydney, Australia.

what I remember of my hometown.' See America, but first see Norristown. I made that up."

Lasorda's godson by extension, Mike Piazza, was born in Norristown but spent his youth playing baseball in Phoenixville, just across the Schuylkill River in Chester County.

Family ties being what they are, the Dodgers selected Mike Piazza in the 1988 draft, although it was in the sixty-second round. Piazza didn't let the late pick bother him one bit, as he went on to become the 1993 MLB Rookie of the Year and eventually broke Carlton Fisk's record for most home runs by a catcher, ending his career with 427.

Lasorda simply convinced the Los Angeles Dodgers powers that be to give Piazza a chance. Piazza had already paid his dues, playing minor league ball in the Dominican Republic and Mexico. He played on five different minor league teams and finally got his shot in the "Big Show" at the age of twenty-four, where he proceeded to prove his mettle by batting nearly .500 in spring training.

Basketball

Basketball fans will remember the name Geno Auriemma for years to come. Perhaps the most prolific coach in women's college basketball, Auriemma called Norristown home from the age of seven, when his family migrated from Montella, Italy. Auriemma went to Bishop Kenrick Catholic High School, which is now Kennedy Kenrick Catholic High School and will soon become Pope John Paul II High School when it merges with St. Pius X and moves to Upper Providence Township, leaving Norristown without a Catholic high school for the first time in generations. Auriemma has coached the University of Connecticut women's basketball program to an impressive thirty-plus wins in thirteen seasons. He has had only one losing season in his twenty-two-year career with the Huskies, and that was the first year he took over the program in 1985. Auriemma has been inducted into the Basketball Hall of Fame in Springfield, Massachusetts, and into the Women's Basketball Hall of Fame in Knoxville, Tennessee.

The game was introduced to Norristown at the turn of the twentieth century by the YMCA. Norristown High School started a team soon after and played its games at Gotwals Elementary School. There was a wire screen between the spectators and the court, giving the gym the nickname the Cage, and players were then dubbed Cagers. For reasons unknown, organizers believed that the audience had to be protected from the players and the ball. When professional basketball was organized, the tradition continued. Norristown basketball aficionados will also remember the Williams brothers. Jim and Henry Williams both were forces to be reckoned with. Henry went on to play basketball at Jacksonville University and was drafted by the New York Knicks. He played in the ABA for the Utah Stars.

Boxing

Boxing has a storied past in Norristown as well. At the turn of the twentieth century, Joe Lenhart was a prominent figure in Norristown's boxing world, training Frank "Fats" Picharuce, Lad Evans, Willie Straub and Frankie McKeever. Coming on their heels were the Cisco brothers, Tony and Hank, along with Al Coulon, Doc DiAngelo and Jimmy and Richie DiCerio.

Perhaps no other Norristown resident has done more to promote boxing than current ambassador of Norristown, Frank "Hank Cisco" Ciaccio. "My brother Tony was ranked fourth in the world as a welterweight," Cisco said. "He fought three world champions. His manager was Chris Dundee, Angelo's brother."

Sergeant Cisco, as he his known to thousands of students who went through the Norristown school system and listened to him lecture on crosswalk safety, was born in Brooklyn, New York. His family moved to Norristown when he was five years old. Cisco recalled,

> *My brother was boxing when he was fourteen years old. He would work out in a garage on Chestnut Street. I used to help out putting the gloves on him, and then I started boxing. The first amateur fight I had was in Chester. The newspaper down there was sponsoring a boxing tournament and I entered. I made it to the finals and lost in a decision. I fought in the Golden Gloves tournament in Philadelphia and came in second there. Coming from a small town, if you wanted to win you had to knock someone out.*

Cisco said that his brother Tony was the real boxer in the family. "He would go into a ring and win a fight just by taking his robe off," Cisco said.

When Cisco was in the Golden Gloves tournament in Philadelphia, he had won about three or four fights to make it to the finals. In one of the bouts, Cisco said that he was going up against a much more experienced

Hank Cisco, at right, and his brother Tony were boxing brothers. Hank, whose real name is Frank Ciaccio, is a Norristown icon and currently holds the position of ambassador of Norristown. *Courtesy of Frank Ciaccio.*

fighter and he wanted to pull out, but his other brother, Joe, told him that he was going to fight the guy; he wasn't going to lose the fight in the dressing room. Cisco said that when the fight started the guy came out swinging but he was too wild and overanxious. After the first round, Joe told him to keep doing what he was doing because it was working. By the third round, Cisco had enough confidence to go out and win the fight.

That night sparked one of his most famous sayings: "I never lost a fight in the dressing room."

Frank Ciaccio grew up on Chestnut Street, between Swede and DeKalb Streets, before moving to Green Street. The family also lived for a short time on Lafayette Street, between Noble and Stanbridge, and on Marshall Street.

Cisco went to New York to pursue his boxing career. By then, his brother Tony, who was about ten years older than Hank, had retired.

"We used the name Cisco because no one could pronounce Ciaccio," Cisco recalled. "Charlie Goldman, the trainer for Rocky Marciano, gave me a tryout and liked what he saw." Hank Cisco had six pro fights before hanging up his gloves for good.

While he'll be the first to admit he took that a lot of shots to the head, Cisco remembers well growing up in Norristown:

> *When we lived on Marshall Street, we were right next to the Holy Saviour School. When I was growing up I wanted to go to St. Patricks but I couldn't because I was Italian. I had to go to Holy Saviour.*
>
> *Growing up we had a group of guys that made up a baseball team. We called ourselves the Belmont. We saw a sign about the races and we picked it as a name for our team. We used to take the scores down to and they would put them in. We got beat so bad once that we changed our name.*

Cisco is somewhat of the epitome of the alternative name culture of his era:

> *Most everybody had nicknames. One guy was Snubber Burns, I don't know where he got the name. Another guy was called Blackie Wilmer, but he wasn't black. Chubby DeFelice was very thin. I don't know where he got that name. Juice Byrnes was another one, I don't know where that came from. My brother Jimmy wanted me to get him a handkerchief one day. I didn't want to do it and he kept yelling at me to get him a hankie. Next thing I know, he's calling me Hank.*

When Cisco was called up to go to war, he said he took the P&W to Allentown to get his physical but he was turned away because he had a perforated eardrum. He received a 4F, meaning he wasn't physically able to serve. A few weeks later, Cisco was boxing in the Golden Gloves tournament in Philadelphia, and his picture was in the paper when he made it to the finals. A few days later, he received a call from the draft board telling him that he was indeed fit enough to serve.

Cisco said that people would sit out on their steps in the evenings because nobody had air conditioners. Growing up, Cisco said he didn't get into too much trouble, possibly because there were six police officers living on his block, including the chief of police, although he doesn't credit them for his career choice.

"When I went to school at Rittenhouse Junior High School I was on the safety patrol, and then I became the head of the safety patrol," said Cisco. "I think that might have had something to do with it. I always had an urge to help people, too."

An ad in the paper for police officers changed Cisco's life. He applied and was accepted. He only had an eighth-grade education, but that was all that was needed back then. He was sworn in and was given a gun and a badge and a nightstick. There wasn't any training. After about ten years on the job, Cisco went back to school and eventually received a degree from Montgomery County Community College, graduating in the first class at the new school. Cisco continued his walk down memory lane:

The Grand Theater looked more like an opera house. It had seats on the side and a balcony. It was beautiful inside. I remember a theatre called the Lyric, right about where the county parking lot is now. The Garrick was on Main Street between Barbadoes and Markley. The Gloria was at Main and Arch, and then it became the Tower. It became known as the Stinks. On Saturdays they would have a special, for five cents you could get a ticket and a candy bar. They would have two shows. The kids wouldn't leave after the first show. If they got up to leave someone would take their seat so they would just pee right on the floor.

Norristonians will remember Frank "Sergeant Cisco" "Hank Cisco" "The Rock" Ciaccio from his days going from class to class teaching students about safety. He would always talk about the proper way for children to cross the street when going to and from school.

Track and Field

Perhaps no other sport has brought more worldwide acclaim to Norristown than track and field. During the 1950s and early '60s, Leroy "Pete" Lewis nurtured the young talent of Norristown High School, leading the team to six PIAA state championships. There have been a number of prolific runners in Norristown's track and field history, but none more so than Josh Culbreath.

Culbreath was a world record holder in hurdles, setting the mark of 50.5 seconds in the 440 in Oslo, Norway, in 1957. Al Cantello was the field star at the time, setting his own world record in the Javelin throw in 1959 in Compton, California, with a toss of 282 feet, 3½ inches. Cantello competed in the 1960 Olympics in Rome, Italy. He went on to a distinguished coaching career at Navy, where he established an impressive 238–68–1 record.

Culbreath competed in the Summer Olympics in 1956 in Melbourne, Australia, but he was already a star, winning three straight national championships in the 440-yard hurdles in 1953, 1954 and 1955 as well as winning the Penn Relays those same three years. He went on to win the bronze medal in the 400-meter hurdles in the Melbourne Olympics. Culbreath recalled his trip down under from his home in Las Vegas:

It was something. I tried to prepare myself for it. I read books about Jesse Owens. I got to know him. I'm still on his board in Chicago. Jesse was an inspiration. He was one of the emissaries. He went to Melbourne with us. People like him and Joe Lewis were people we looked up to. When he talked to me, I was the shortest hurdler in the world, but I was ranked number one in the world. Yuri Liteyev was ranked number one in the world in the metric system.

Culbreath said that he was on the first USA versus USSR team to visit the communist country:

The first time we went there was in 1958. It was the first time a team went behind the iron curtain. The first time they came to America, it was 1959. All the Big Five coaches picked my teammate to win and me to get last. They all picked Dickey Howard to win. My coach, Edward T. Hurt, from Morgan State, picked me to win. Dickey and I ran the eighth, ninth and tenth hurdles together, and then I just took off. It was held at Franklin Field at the University of Pennsylvania.

Glenn Davis was the only man in the world to beat Culbreath more times than he beat him. "He whipped me four times," said Culbreath with a bit of a chuckle in his voice, "and he had to break the world record to do it."

Culbreath said he was never defeated by a European and never defeated in South America, but he was defeated in Africa by a man from Pretoria.

He was a policeman. It was the first time a black man ran against a white man in South Africa. We were sponsored by the United States Information Service, the USIS. We had a pole vaulter, Don Garsenbrag, he was the gold medalist in the 1960 Olympics. Robert Gardner was a high jumper from St. Johns. Perry O'Brien had competed in Nigeria but he had to go back. Ira Davis was from Lasalle College. He was a triple jumper. He was a three-time Olympian. It was a five-man team. The coach was Carl Olsen from the University of Pittsburgh.

Culbreath likened the experience in South Africa to that of Martin Luther King Jr. and recalled his time working in the civil rights movement while at Morgan State. "We didn't have an entourage," said Culbreath. "They tried to start an incident. Ira and I went into a white barbershop and tried to get a haircut. I said if these people decide to take a shot at us we're in trouble."

But even halfway across the world, Culbreath was an ambassador for civil rights, and he found his counterpart of a different color carrying on the same struggle in a different land.

"Zerharduf Potgetier was a wonderful athlete," Culbreath said. "There were three of them who wanted to integrate. They were breaking apartheid law. Apartheid made the Ku Klux Klan look like a babe in the woods. It was fifty years ago this last March." Culbreath said he wanted to go back to South Africa to mark the anniversary but couldn't make the trip.

As he began to recall his days growing up in Norristown, Culbreath remembered:

Norristown is where it all began to get to Melbourne. Rittenhouse Junior High School is where it actually started. We're talking about the '40s now. I was on the track team when I was in seventh grade. I couldn't buy a race. I was on the eighty-five-pound team. I was the fifth guy on the wheel. They wanted to win, but they didn't think they could win with me. Mr. Burger said they were going to use Inky Wagner. His name was Robert, but his nickname was Inky. Inky wanted to give me the medal he won the year before. I told him I didn't want his, I wanted my own.

It wasn't long before Culbreath's love affair with the hurdles began to take root:

Josh Culbreath (left) was a world record holder in hurdles, setting the mark of 50.5 seconds in the 440 in Oslo, Norway, in 1957. He's seen here with "Skag" Cottman and Jesse Owens at a sports banquet in Philadelphia. *Courtesy of the Skag Cottman family.*

We had a little strip in the back of Rittenhouse. It was cinder. I taught myself how to run. No one taught me. I taught myself. By the time I was in eighth grade I became very versatile. I was running the hurdles in a meet, but yet I won the pole vault. I had an old bamboo pole. We would land on shavings. We didn't have the big, nice soft place to land that they have today.

Culbreath didn't run on the track team his first year in high school because the coach wanted him to compete in the pole vault. He said he wanted to run the hurdles and actually defeated the team's top runners in an impromptu race that he ran barefoot, but the coach had made up his mind.

Culbreath said that when he returned to the team the next year the coach called him over and said he wanted him to stay on the team that year. "My senior year, I said I wasn't going to let anyone get close to me," Culbreath recalled. "I think I ran the second fastest time in the country for the two-hundred-yard low hurdles. May 19, 1951, I hit the ninth hurdle, rolled over and then high jumped over the tenth hurdle and still took third place. If hadn't hit that ninth hurdle I probably would have set a record."

Culbreath also played football in high school. "Some people think I was a better football player than I was a runner," Culbreath said. Charles Blockson was the fullback on the football team. He went on to play at Penn State with Lenny Moore and Rosie Greer. Like Culbreath, Blockson was a multi-sport athlete. Blockson ran the lead leg in the mile relay, Joseph Hadrick was second, Culbreath ran third and John Willie Spearman ran the anchor. "We won it two years in a row and we had a shot putter leading off," Culbreath said of Blockson. "He was collecting artifacts when he was eight and nine years old," Culbreath said of the soon to become nationally renowned historian. "People thought he was crazy back then, but I had faith in him."

Josh Culbreath was born in Norristown in 1932. He traveled the world with his talent and settled in Las Vegas, Nevada, but his recollection of Norristown is still vivid. He recalled:

> We had an international group of people in Norristown. They couldn't pronounce all of the names of the streets or towns. Alan Wood had a little town, it was called Connaughtown. They called it Cullytown because they couldn't pronounce it.
>
> Mogeetown, there was a quarry there. I learned how to swim in that quarry. It was dangerous, but we didn't know anyone to drown down there.

Culbreath said that he learned a lot from the guys he hung out with as a child, including Tommy Lasorda, Charles Blockson and Jimmy Smith.

> We had so many different nationalities on our block. It was a wonderful environment in which we grew. We knew who the people were in our neighborhood.
>
> At Chestnut and Arch they called it Frog Hollow. There were small houses there, maybe two or three rooms. That went from Oak almost to Marshall. Those were little homes.
>
> We have some great history in Norristown. I can speak on it with a lot of enthusiasm. I grew up on Walnut Street, between Oak and Marshall in an interracial neighborhood. Across the street from my home, at the corner of Marshall and Chestnut, was Holy Saviour School. Tommy Lasorda lived right there at the end of that alley. Tommy grew up about six doors from me. We were children together. He was the same age as my older

brother. Tommy and I, we still have dinner together when he hits Vegas. We've never forgotten where we came from. We share an expression, "We were so poor that we didn't even know we were poor."

Culbreath said jazz great Jimmy Smith's younger brother was a great athlete. "Clarence Smith is a name people who know about athletics back in those days will remember," Culbreath said.

Where I lived on Walnut Street we had to go to Washington Street , and then Welsh and then back to Washington. Later I went to Hancock. I went to three of them before I went to Rittenhouse. They were all overcrowded with people.

Coming from little Norristown is something. I'm surprised when I come back home. I can still tell you where we had the three theatres, the Garrick, the Grand and the Towers. All of these were vaudeville theatres that were converted to movies. That's quite a little town. We were the largest little borough, someone said at one time, in the world.

Culbreath's father, like many fathers in Norristown, worked at Alan Wood Steel. Josh Culbreath also put in a few years at the formidable steel plant. "I became one of the first blacks in the personnel department there," he said. "If you counted up the Culbreaths that worked there, my father had forty years of service, I was there about six years. With all the uncles and such I counted up more than two hundred years of service for the Culbreath family at Alan Wood Steel."

Culbreath said that he was the first black to teach in secondary schools in Norristown at Rittenhouse Junior High. "Mr. Vincent Farina, when he became the principal at Rittenhouse, he wanted me to come teach there," said Culbreath. "He was my history teacher. He was also my second track coach, with Abraham Burger being my first track coach in junior high school."

Culbreath said there were no racial problems growing up in Norristown:

Papa Sabatini Lasorda spoke broken English. My father wasn't educated. They had a great relationship.

When I talked to Tommy and Jimmy Smith, we never asked each other what we wanted to be when we grew up. We just played. We would take a baseball and beat it to death. We would take tape, any kind of tape, just to wrap it up. We had a big open field at Basin and Violet Streets called Blue

Mill Field. This is what the colored people used for baseball at the time. I use "colored" because that's what they used at the time. It wasn't where we had to go, it was convenient. You had no other open fields at the time. We played baseball right in the street. We'd use a mop stick and try to hit a ball about the size of a golf ball.

They had a riding academy there. You could rent a horse and ride it. They didn't have all the homes that are there now.

While delving in nearly every sport as a youth, Culbreath had track and field to thank for taking him around the world.

Just as fast, but not nearly as lucky, Norristown's second brush with Olympic gold was never to be. Speedster Tony Darden was on the Olympic team in 1980 when President Jimmy Carter boycotted the Olympic games.

Darden started winning races early in life and never looked back. He set the national scholastic record in the three-hundred-yard dash with a time of 30.6-seconds at Princeton University. He set another national record in the four-hundred-yard dash in Knoxville, Tennessee, with a time of 45.7 seconds.

By the time he made it to college, he was outrunning nearly everyone he lined up against. He was the two-time defending champion in the 440-yard hurdles at the Philadelphia Track Classic in 1980 when he ran for a third straight title. He won the National Sports Festival 400-meter race in Colorado with a 45.02 time.

He also won the Pan-American games in the same race, clocked at 45.11 seconds, but more importantly, he beat Cuba's Alberto Juantorena, the gold medal winner in the 1976 Montreal Olympics, and fellow countryman Willie Smith, ranked numbers one and two, respectively.

Tennis

The tennis world and its fans will know the name Lisa Raymond. Raymond was born on August 10, 1973, in Norristown. She has wins over the likes of Venus Williams, Martina Hingis and Monica Seles. She has four titles to her own, two coming in the Cellular South Cup in Memphis, Tennessee. Raymond became an accomplished doubles player, winning a career grand slam. Although she has spent her career traveling the world playing in tournaments like Wimbledon, Raymond still lives in the area, in Wayne, and plays for the Philadelphia Freedoms in King of Prussia–hosted World Team Tennis tournament in July.

Tony Darden was a standout track athlete at Norristown Area High School and Arizona State University. Darden was set to run in the 1980 Olympics before President Jimmy Carter called for a boycott.

Lisa Raymond has wins over some of tennis's most prolific female players, including Serena Williams and Monica Seles.

The Names of Norristown

Her career started at an early age, as it often does with tennis players. In 1990, she was the number one ranked player under eighteen years of age. She went on to the University of Florida, where she won singles titles in 1992 and 1993. She was named the collegiate player of the year in 1992.

LITERARY FIGURES

One of Norristown's most famous literary sons has a penchant for the people and places he would encounter and explore while growing up. Jerry Spinelli, author of twenty-five books, including *Maniac Magee*, a Newbery Medal winner, said he wanted to be a baseball player growing up and really had no idea that his hometown would later play a major role in his writing. He was born on February 1, 1941, in Norristown. He remembered:

> *Riding around on my cream and green Roadmaster, I had no idea I was compiling memories that I would call on years later. I do remember riding my bicycle and feeling that I had connections to all parts of town. I remember being impressed even at a young age that Norristown seemed to be a small Philadelphia. It seemed to have a little of everything. I used to like to click off its assets. It had four theatres. The Garrick, the Grand, the Norris and the West-Mar.*
>
> *It had two downtowns. It had the main downtown, with the theatres and department stores, like Blocks, and it had another downtown on West Marshall Street. That's where the West-Mar was.*

Spinelli recalled his father's home on East Chestnut Street and the garden his father kept, even though Spinelli never saw it growing up:

> *He and his goombas had plots down there. He liked to say he was going to work on his farm. I never actually saw it myself until the day of his funeral. The funeral was heading down the street and I noticed that it wasn't headed to the cemetery, it was headed down through the East End. They were paying homage to his East Chestnut Street home and his farm.*

Norristown was and still is made up of three distinct sections of town. Spinelli said that in his day the West End was mostly blue collar. The East End was more ethnic. You could see Italian families playing bocce in

Jerry Spinelli credits the *Norristown Times Herald* with launching his career after a poem he wrote about a Norristown versus Lower Merion football game appeared in the sports pages.

their backyards, Spinelli recalled. The North End was considered more prosperous. Spinelli recalled, with a hint of facetiousness in his voice:

> *The big homes up there had things like front yards and driveways and they had things under the living rooms called basements, not cellars. There was a sense that you could work your way up from the East End to the West End to the North End.*
>
> *I liked that we had our own park. And we had our own zoo. How many towns could claim that? I recall there was a lion and bears. There were cool monkeys. I would go exploring along the town's own river, the Stony Creek.*
>
> *I would explore the state hospital grounds. It was like a small city. It's hard to believe that we were ushered into a small room and saw a pig dunked into a vat of boiling water. The state hospital was a lot different then. It was campus. There were upward of four thousand people there. I worked there as a psychiatric aide one summer. They were popularly called attendants, but the instructor told us we should consider ourselves psychiatric aides. I worked in Building 6, I believe it was. They produced their own food, grew their own vegetables.*

Today, only a handful of buildings are occupied on the state hospital grounds.

Spinelli had dreams of being a big league baseball player when he was growing up, but it was a Norristown High School football game that changed his life forever:

> *The occasion was a major football game at Roosevelt Field. It was Norristown against Lower Merion. Lower Merion was one of the top teams in the country. If there was a back then they would have had them as one of the top twenty-five teams. They had won thirty-two straight games over a period of three years. They were playing Norristown at Roosevelt Field on a Friday night. We were actually beating them, 7–6, thanks to a partially blocked extra point. I was up in the stands watching. I was on the soccer team. The game was almost over when one of their players got loose on an end-around. He made it all the way to the one-yard line. Of course, it didn't occur to them to pass. They bulled straight away four straight times and we stopped them every time. We won the game 7–6. Of course, the place went wild. Horns were blasting. While the town was celebrating, I went home and wrote that poem in long hand. I had a sense even then that someone needed to memorialize that day. I gave it to my father*

and didn't think much about it after that. A couple of days later, I opened the . I went straight to the sports pages because that's all I read back then. What I didn't know was that my father had taken the poem to his friend, Red McCarthy; I'm sure you know that name. Right there in the middle of a page was my poem.

That was the beginning of my junior year. By the time I graduated high school, I decided I was going to be a writer. I traded in my baseball bat for a pen.

That 1957 poem, Spinelli's first published work, appeared in *The Times Herald* on October 16, 1957.

Obviously, Spinelli went on to publish many more works and is still writing today. One of his most popular, *Maniac Magee*, was based on Spinelli's early days in Norristown. "Norristown becomes Two Mills in my fiction. I was born on Fornance Street. We moved to Chestnut Street. We made it to the West End, 802 George Street. If you make a list of all the features of the town, you have a very impressive place, and I knew it as well as anybody and perhaps in some inarticulate way appreciated it."

When asked to describe his memories of Norristown, Spinelli said it had everything.

It's kind of hard to put into words. I think of its diversity and variety. I think of it as a little Philadelphia. As a place I didn't have to leave. I could go exploring in the afternoon and attend a movie that night. There was a little bit of everything.

The train that used to come through. I've described that in . It was a frightening thing. Laying in my bed on George Street, I would hear this faint chugging. I knew what was coming. In a few minutes it was as if the universe was exploding. I would go outside the next morning and if my mother had left the wash out overnight it would be covered with soot from the locomotive.

We would take the train into Philadelphia. At the terminal at Markley and Elm, there were two train lines to chose from. There was the Pennsylvania train and the Reading. If we were going into Philadelphia we would take the Reading line with its blue seats. They were scratchy like they were made out of Brillo pads.

In a sense, I didn't move away from Norristown for quite a while, unless you count the time at college and the naval reserves. I was away at Baltimore when I got my master's at Johns Hopkins. I eventually came back to town, lived with my folks for a while, got an apartment on the West End, West Main Street. I was in my thirties when I got married and moved to Havertown.

When asked about his old hometown, Spinelli becomes a bit nostalgic. "I guess I miss the sense that here was this complete world. A place where I could walk down to Texas Hot Wieners and get a hot dog. The little things like that." While the owners have changed over the years, Montgomery Lunch is still in business and still serving the famous Texas Hot Wieners.

Charles L. Blockson, Norristown's most notable bibliophile, is a historian and author and has amassed one of the world's largest collections of African American culture, which is now housed at Temple University. And yes, he's the same Blockson Josh Culbreath referred to earlier in these pages.

He was born on December 16, 1933, to Ann and Charles E. Blockson and developed pneumonia and scarlet fever while a young child. This was certainly not the most promising start for a soon-to-be star athlete. Blockson excelled in both football and track and field. He ran the first leg in the mile relay on Culbreath's team and threw the shot put as well. He excelled in football and track and field and went on to compete in both at Penn State. He was offered a contract to play with the New York Giants but turned them down. He soon enlisted in the army, but his love of books simply could not be denied. He returned to Norristown briefly to teach in the Norristown Area School District, and was the first to be inducted into the Norristown Area High School Hall of Fame, Hall of Champions.

Wanderlust would soon get the best of him, and he traveled the world in search of African American artifacts, teaching African American and Afro-centric history along the way. He eventually donated his massive collection to Temple University and became the curator of the Charles L. Blockson Afro-American collection. He is the author of eleven books, including his autobiography, *Damn Rare: The Memoirs of an African American Bibliophile*.

With his world travels and extensive writings, it would be easy to understand if Blockson's memories of his days growing up in Norristown would be fading at this stage in his life, but they remain crystal clear. One incident in particular stands out in his mind. The George Washington Carver Community Center in Norristown was built after a tragic accident, and Blockson remembers it well.

"We had to learn to swim in the Schuylkill River or Stony Creek," Blockson said. Blacks were not allowed to swim in the pool at the YMCA. "Delores's

Charles Blockson has amassed perhaps the largest collection of African American artifacts in the world. His collection is housed at Temple University.

brother, Stanley, and one of the Johnson girls were caught in a whirlpool in Stony Creek," Blockson said. The tragic accident occurred in the late 1950s.

"They marched on city hall. We demanded a place to swim," Blockson said. "Harry Butera, Bob's father, led the way to build the Carver Community Center." The center has served the black community since those early days, but funding always seems to be an issue.

Although athletics propelled Blockson to Penn State, academics and history have always been his passion. Blockson recalls, as a boy, marching to Valley Forge to the Boy Scout Jamboree. "Never did I know, years later, because of my research, I never knew that African Americans were at the encampment at Valley Forge during the Revolution. From a young boy as a Boy Scout, my name is now on a monument in the park. It was put there by the Delta Theta sorority."

His stunning and promising career as an athlete always took a back seat to his love of history, and as you talk to him today that love comes in staccato bursts of impeccable recollection. *Damn Rare* is a book that Blockson refers to often.

The George Washington Carver Community Center was built after two black teens drowned while swimming in Stony Creek. Blacks were not allowed to swim in the pool at the YMCA. *Courtesy of the author.*

"I was always proud to say I came from Norristown. Aside from the hurt and pain of segregation, I've always been proud of Norristown. I used to play football and run track and feel the elation, and then you would feel the stigmatism of segregation. Things have changed. There are still areas of racism. With Obama now president, though, things are changing."

ENTERTAINERS

While there have been a few people from Norristown who have gone on to fame and fortune in the entertainment world—Peter Boyle comes quickly to mind—no one made more of an impact in a single field than jazz great Jimmy Smith. And while the town is by no means finished producing legends, it is well worth noting here that Smith grew up with several of the most notable Norristonians, including track great Josh Culbreath and baseball's very own ambassador, Tom Lasorda.

Jimmy Smith set the jazz world on fire when he took the once benign Hammond organ and turned it into a jazz instrument. When he wasn't playing ball with Josh Culbreath, he was teaching himself how to play piano, and at the tender age of eight he won the Major Bowes Children's Talent Show. He went on to study music at the Hamilton School of Music and Ornstein School of Music from 1948 to 1950. With formal training under his belt, Jimmy Smith said goodbye to Norristown and traveled the world, later returning to form the Jimmy Smith Quartet.

When Smith passed away in 2005, *The Times Herald* spoke with his sister, Anita Johnson. "There have been some before him," Johnson said. "But none like him."

Johnson had last seen her brother just a few weeks earlier at the Iridium Club in New York. "The crowd went crazy. The line was around the block all the way to Broadway. If we weren't family we wouldn't have gotten in. People sat and watched him in awe. The old people that have been following him for the better part of sixty years would still come to wherever he was."

Even at that age, in his late seventies, Jimmy Smith was still traveling the world. Johnson said that her brother was booked through the end of the summer that year and had just returned from Spain, Germany and Japan.

While Smith traveled the world, Norristown has hosted celebrities since the days before it was established as a borough. Perhaps this country's first celebrity, General George Washington, stopped in Norristown in 1794 as he was making his way across the county, according to *Southeastern*

The Names of Norristown

Pennsylvania, a History of the Counties of Berks, Bucks, Chester, Delaware, Montgomery, Philadelphia and Schuylkill, edited by J. Bennett Nolan. The remainder of this chapter will recount other prominent visitors to Norristown, as recounted in Nolan's book.

Washington was in Montgomery County the previous year due to a yellow fever outbreak in Philadelphia, then the country's capital, scouting for a spot to possibly host Congress. The outbreak subsided, however, and Congress convened in Philadelphia that year.

President James Buchanan would visit Norristown on occasion after his presidency to discuss business with John B. Sterigere. Buchanan was also present at Sterigere's funeral in 1852.

President Grover Cleveland was picked up at the Norristown station for the Pennsylvania Railroad by William M. Singerly, publisher of the *Philadelphia Record* and a prominent Democrat, and was driven by carriage to Singerly's farm on DeKalb Street, at the intersection of Morris Road.

President Theodore Roosevelt was in the area on several occasions and stopped in Norristown while traveling by train while campaigning for office. Roosevelt was a descendant of the local Lukens and Tyson families and often referred to them in his speeches.

Former president William Howard Taft delivered a speech at city hall in Norristown in support of the fundraising efforts of the YMCA.

Horace Greeley lectured at the Odd Fellows Hall in Norristown on November 26, 1855, and the occasion was captured in the *Norristown Herald*, describing Greeley as wearing a long gray coat, short tight pants and large rough boots. The *Herald* stated that while the lecture was "highly instructive and amusing, [it] was indifferently delivered."

Norristown's Odd Fellows Hall also hosted Samuel L. Clemens on October 25, 1871, at a cost of $150 for the privilege of hearing "Mark Twain" speak on "Reminiscences of Some Uncommon People I Have Met." However, the lecture was apparently not popular with earlier audiences, so Clemens spent the evening speaking on Artemus Ward, a popular American humorist of the time. Unfortunately for Clemens, his hastily prepared speech contained anecdotes about Ward, most of which had previously appeared in the *Norristown Herald*.

PART III

The People
of Norristown

W hile the early settlers were mostly English of Quaker persuasion, Norristown boasted, and still does, one of the most diverse populations in the county. When the Town of Norris was just beginning to gain footing, there were Pennsylvania Germans, Welsh, Dutch and Swedes walking its dusty streets, but by the middle of the nineteenth century the Irish began flocking into Norristown, attracted by the lure of solid pay for a good day's labor. The Irish were fleeing horrible conditions in their homeland, and by the end of the century Italians, mostly from the Sciacca region of Sicily and Montella in the Campania region of central Italy, began to transform the East End. In the mid- to late 1990s, Norristown experienced another influx of immigrants as its Hispanic population, most coming from Mexico, grew by leaps and bounds, beginning with a small contingent from Puerto Rico. As with the Italian immigrants, the Mexican immigrants came mostly from two cities, Puebla and Acapulco.

The Irish

The Irish quickly went to work building canals and railroads as they arrived during the early years of Norristown's growth. However, there were no Catholic churches in Norristown. Those of the Catholic faith in Norristown had to travel to Manayunk to worship. After a Catholic church was established there about 1830, missionary efforts began in Norristown. Some services were held in the homes of Norristown's Catholic population. A news article in the *Norristown Herald* in November 1832 declared that "the Rev. Charles I.H. Carter, a Catholic clergyman from Manayunk, by permission of the vestry, will preach in St. John's [Episcopal] Church, Norristown, Sunday afternoon, Nov. 11 at 3 p.m."

From St. Patrick Parish would grow Holy Saviour Parish in 1903, which was started by a group of Italian Catholics who first worshiped at the second home of St. Patrick at Lafayette and Cherry Streets. St. Francis Parish was established in 1923 in the West End of Norristown, and St. Paul's Parish was established just across Johnson Highway in the North End in East Norriton Township.

Bishop Kenrick gave permission in 1834 to start a parish in Norristown, and construction on the first St. Patrick Church was completed in 1839 at Washington and Cherry Streets. The parish would soon outgrow its first home, and a new church was built at Lafayette and Cherry Streets in 1864.

Ironically, some of the same Irish worshiping in the church were also laying the railroad that would travel directly in front of the church, leading to an eventual lawsuit and the church being granted enough money to build anew in the 700 block of DeKalb Street, where St. Patrick still stands today.

While the Italian Catholics have long held a monopoly on feasts throughout Norristown, the Irish gave a gallant effort in 1994, when St. Patrick Church held its first ever Irish Festival. The Feast of Our Lady of Knock was a huge success. The festival was held to carry on the tradition from County Mayo in Ireland, honoring the vision of the Blessed Mother, St. Joseph and St. John the Evangelist.

The Italians

About a half century later, at the turn of the twentieth century, Italians began migrating to Norristown. By now, industry was booming in Norristown and there was plenty of work for the entire family, especially in the textile mills, where children often were employed. Most of the Italian immigrants, many from Sicily and particularly the Sciacca region, settled into the East End of town. The Italian immigrants also found steady work, mostly in construction and in factories. The women also found work in the many textile mills in Norristown.

It wasn't long, however, before enterprising immigrants were starting their own businesses. Rocco Borzillo traveled to Norristown from New

York, where he found work in the brickyards, according to a story by his daughter, Mary Borzillo Pallandino. Borzillo emigrated from Benevento, Italy, in 1892 and made his way to Norristown in 1903. After being here for just a short time, Borzillo purchased a small piece of property at 511 East Lafayette Street and opened a small grocery store. His wife was making bread one day and Borzillo suggested that she should sell the bread to all of their friends. Borzillo built a small open hearth oven in their basement and later bought a horse and wagon to deliver the bread. In 1913, he built his bakery at Main and Walnut Streets and continued to deliver his bread by horse and wagon. In 1924, he bought five trucks and encouraged his relatives to come here and learn to drive so they could have jobs delivering the bread. Rocco Borzillo died in 1942, but the bakery thrived for many years, eventually selling out to Amoroso's in 1972 so they could concentrate on specialty cookies and wafers.

The Italians were quick to establish places of worship, which also included social clubs. Holy Saviour Parish was established in 1903 and is still going strong today, even though Holy Saviour School was recently combined with Our Lady of Victory in East Norriton Township.

However, before the S.S. Salvatore Church was constructed, the Italian population attended services at the "Irish" church, the original St. Patrick at Cherry and Lafayette, as it was the only Catholic church in Norristown at the time.

When the Italian population began to swell, plans were put into place to build a church of their own. The S.S. Salvatore Church still stands today, although you won't be able to see it unless you venture inside Holy Saviour Catholic Church at Main and Walnut Streets.

When the church was dedicated on September 20, 1903, a story appeared in the *Norristown Herald* describing it as:

> *an odd looking little church which is only a half story high, but adorned with a belfry. The church, though uncompleted, presents the appearance of a finished edifice. The illusion as to its size is lost when one enters the structure. A large auditorium is opened to view with a high altar, ample sanctuary and a choir loft with pipe organ. The building here is really the basement of what will be, when completed, one of the finest cut stone churches in town.*

By the next year, the first of many Italian clubs was born. The Societa di Mutuo Soccorso Maria SS. Del Soccorso de Sciacca was formed to

Borzillo Bakery was a mainstay in Norristown for many years, solidifying the image of an immigrant making good in America.

serve the immigrants from Sciacca, Sicily. The societies were formed to support members from certain regions in Italy. Two years later, in 1906, what is now known as the Holy Saviour Club was formed by a group from Montella, in the region of Campania. The Societa di M.S. del SS. Salvatore counted among its founding members Rocco Borzillo, of Borzillo Bakery fame.

The names of the founding members of the Italian clubs are virtually a who's who of Norristown's past. Names like Bello, Santangelo and Romano are still found on boards and letterheads throughout town.

Nearly five years to the day after the dedication of the "basement church," members of Holy Saviour Parish gathered together on September 21, 1908, for the blessing of the new church at Main and Walnut Streets, and once again a forerunner of *The Times Herald* was there: "There were several thousand persons who tried to gain admission to the church and [Norristown police] Chief Rodenbaugh and his squad of policemen had considerable trouble in preventing an accident."

The new church was described as:

> *a plain, but pleasing structure, measuring 50 by 100 feet. The walls are of granite. The seating capacity is six hundred. The furnishings are of oak, including the altar, which were carved at the Catholic Protectory, and which reflect high credit upon the instructors and youthful artisans of that institution. The edifice is provided with a choir loft and organ and the illumination is by gas and electricity. Practically all the furnishings are gifts from friends of the zealous pastor.*

The Holy Saviour Club remains one of the most active today, and still carries on the traditional of an annual feast in celebration of the society.

African Americans

While Norristown is the home of one of America's foremost leading authorities on African American culture and history, it has shared the same segregation that most towns, North and South, shared during the early years of our country. Since those early days, Norristown has grown to be a town of great diversity, although many blacks still mark time with the "firsts" that have occurred.

The People of Norristown

Charles L. Blockson, noted historian and collector, recounted some of the firsts to occur in Norristown.

> *Hank Simmons became the first black councilman. The first African American woman to ever teach in Norristown was Mary Ann Shadd. They asked her to come and teach at the colored schoolhouse. That was where Montgomery Hospital is now. That was before my time. The first African American public schoolteacher was Alice Davenport. Alice Davenport is the wife of Montgomery County's first African American judge, the Honorable Horace Davenport.*

Rochelle Griffin Culbreath became Norristown's first black female council president.

Blockson has traveled the world in search of African and African American artifacts. He has made it his life's work to document and preserve black history. Blockson recalled of Norristown:

> *We always had good schools. It was a tight-knit community where we lived on Lafayette Street. There were Italians, Polish people, Jews, blacks, we always played together. Once we got in high school though, we never had black teachers.*
>
> *One thing I remember and despise was the annual minstrel show at Rittenhouse. There were five theatres in Norristown when I was growing up. The only theatre where we could sit with whites was the Tower Theater. Every other theatre was segregated. We had to sit upstairs at the other theatres. The New York Store on Main Street, we couldn't go there. We couldn't go to the hotel on Main Street. The YMCA, and the YWCA, we were not permitted to become members. That didn't come about until the 1960s.*
>
> *There was a restaurant on Cherry near Penn that had a sign in the window that said we reserve the right to serve whites only. Those things you just don't forget.*

Blockson remembered that very few African Americans who lived in the West End, and blacks were not even allowed to enter the West-Mar Theatre.

"They had the black community at the Mount Zion AME Church," Blockson recalled. "They had several families involved. My family is documented in William Stills book. My family came up from Delaware. You had about three or four [black] families in Norristown at that time."

Through the years, Blockson has learned a lot about people from learning about their past, and he pointed out with some note of pride that Norristown was one of the first towns to protest against segregation, under the leadership of Reverend Amos Wilson of Mount Zion AME Church.

THE LATEST WAVE OF IMMIGRANTS

Much like the wave of immigrants at the turn of the twentieth century, the latest wave to hit Norristown arrived at the turn of the twenty-first century. During the first few years of this century, the Mexican population in Norristown has increased exponentially. While Norristown has had a fledgling Hispanic population for several years, rising approximately 400 percent between 1990 and 2000, there has been a dramatic increase in the number of Mexican immigrants, mostly from two cities, Puebla and Acapulco. By some estimates, there are approximately six thousand Mexican nationals living in Norristown, where the total population hovers around thirty thousand. The latest wave is very similar to that of the early twentieth-century wave of Italian immigrants. Mexican immigrants are coming here in search of a better life. They work hard, and many have started their own businesses and put down roots.

The parallels of the immigration waves are uncanny. Both occurred at the turn of a century, and both occurred due to economic conditions in the homelands. The Irish, who came to these shores more in the middle of the nineteenth century, were fleeing famine and disease. The Italian immigrants came to America in search of a better life, fleeing poor economic conditions. Many of the Italian immigrants came to this country illegally, especially before the United States established Ellis Island, the processing hub for immigrants searching for a better life.

Norristown has become home to the largest concentration of Mexican immigrants in all of Montgomery County. Inexpensive housing could be one of the reasons, as well as the easy access to transportation, which can ferry the immigrants to jobs throughout the region.

There are many legal immigrants of Mexican descent in Norristown today, and a second generation has been started, making language barriers expensive from a social services aspect. Schools in Norristown have to make accommodations for students who don't know the language, and that comes at a cost.

West Marshall Street has become a haven for the Mexican population. Stores and restaurants operated by their country folk line the busy street, catering to their needs and wants. While some of the businesses come and go, there are a few that have established themselves in this area and also along Main Street and Markley Street.

PART IV

THE PLACES
OF NORRISTOWN

Norristown's Elmwood Park Zoo is the most visible attraction in town, but there are other areas to visit. A driving tour of Norristown is a must for anyone interested in architecture, and the renovation of the Selma Mansion will bring a piece of history to life.

SELMA MANSION

While the date of construction cannot be accurately concluded, Selma Mansion, at the convergence of Main and Airy Streets, is most likely the oldest family dwelling in Norristown—although the mansion, when originally built, was located in Norriton Township. Selma Mansion, which likely was built before the formation of the county in 1784, became part of Norristown as the borough expanded in its early years.

When Colonel Andrew Porter, a Revolutionary War officer, bought the property in 1786, there was a house already there. Porter bought the property from Alexander McCaman, described in the deed as a "yeoman" from Norriton Township. McCaman had owned the property since 1770 after purchasing it from Mary Norris, widow of Charles Norris, who was a son of Isaac Norris. The property at the time included 115 acres. Porter lived in the house for many years, most likely until his death in 1813. His heirs eventually sold the property in 1823 to Mrs. Andrew Knox.

According to a published account in *The Times Herald* celebrating the 150th anniversary of the founding of Norristown, Porter's heirs originally tried to sell the property just after the colonel's death, but apparently no sale resulted. A description of the property was contained in the advertisement of the sale:

The stone house, it was set forth, was "large, convenient and elegant," 50 by 36 feet. The stone barn, 80 by 45 feet was also elegant and there was a coach house, granary, wagon house, poultry house, smoke house and milk house, all of stone, the latter standing over a never-failing spring. Further features were a stone tenant house, a fine garden enclosed with a stone wall, a pump of excellent never-failing water within three yards of the kitchen door, 40 acres of woodland, a 12-acre meadow and an orchard.

Andrew and Mary Knox's son, Colonel Thomas P. Knox, lived at Selma from 1851 until his death in 1879. His daughter, Ellen, married Joseph Fornance, a member of the Montgomery Bar and another prominent Norristown family, and the Fornance family then took up residence in the mansion. The property was still owned by the Fornance family in 1962, when the history of Selma was put down in the pages of *The Times Herald*.

Major Joseph Knox Fornance, who was interviewed for the story, was quoted as saying,

According to family tradition the name was taken for the place from one of the poems of Ossian, which had the same title. I believe that the name was given to the place when it was purchased by my great-grandmother, Mrs. Andrew Knox, in 1823. This family tradition is fully borne out by an heirloom in the form of an ancient copy of the poems of Ossian, which contains the poem "Selma" and is inscribed on the flyleaf with my great-grandmother's name.

The mansion has been home to many historic figures, including the mother of Mary Todd Lincoln, wife of President Abraham Lincoln.

The Norristown Preservation Society is taking on the task of restoring the mansion and hopes to open it soon as a museum. A marker has been placed at the edge of the property by the preservation society that reads: "Selma Home of Andrew Porter, Revolutionary War general. Birthplace of his sons: David R., Gov. of Penna., 1839–45; James M., Sec. of War, 1843; George B., Gov. of Michigan Territory, 1831–34."

Selma Mansion is most likely the oldest family dwelling in Norristown although the mansion, when originally built, was located in Norriton Township.

ELMWOOD PARK ZOO

While its history may not be filled with as many famous characters as the Selma Mansion, Elmwood Park has been a part of Norristown since the turn of the twentieth century, when Amos W. Barnes donated a little more than thirty-four acres to the borough. The zoo was carved out of Elmwood Park and consisted of about six acres when it was established in 1924.

One of Elmwood Park Zoo's best friends was Morton "Bubby" Weiss and his wife Lenore. The Weiss family began their love affair with the zoo in the 1960s, when then curator Arthur Herr sent them a solicitation for a donation. The zoo used the $1,800 Weiss donated to buy a zebra. Weiss, who owned Gilberts on Main Street in Norristown, a business started by his father, would go on to serve as president of the zoo's board of directors. Weiss continued to support the zoo throughout the years. In one of his final acts before passing away in 2004, Weiss donated enough funds for the zoo to offer free entrance on the Fourth of July.

Future plans for the zoo are ambitious, with twenty additional acres being donated by the municipality just across Stony Creek. The master plan has four phases that will be implemented during the next two decades at a cost of approximately $60 million. The first phase will include an animal-care and conservation center. The second phase will take the zoo across Stony Creek into a South American exhibit. The third phase will include a jaguar exhibit with a rainforest-style setting. The final phase of the expansion will include a sea lion amphitheatre. The zoo will eventually be connected to the Norristown Farm Park, which straddles Norristown and East and West Norriton, through a connector trail.

Elmwood Park is also home to the Thomas J. Stewart Armory, which was built in 1928, and the Fire Chief's Memorial Band Shell, which was built in 1936 and is still used today for free concerts in the summer. Elmwood Park consists of about one hundred acres and has been developed over the years to include picnic tables, grills for cooking out, bathroom facilities and, more recently, a bocce ball court.

The Columbus Monument is also in Elmwood Park. The monument originally was to be built in 1926 when money was collected to build the monument. Twelve men of Italian heritage went to borough hall to get a tract of land for the monument. The borough gave them a small piece of land at Harding Boulevard and Sterigere Street. John Bolger, a stonemason and grandfather of Montgomery County Common Pleas Court judge Joseph Smyth, placed a small marker that read, "On this site will be erected a monument for Christopher Columbus." With the oncoming Depression, the project was put on hold. However, a marker was placed at the site, with the intention of one day coming back to the project.

In 1984, Frank Ciaccio, a motorcycle patrolman with the Norristown Police Department, came upon the marker. Ciaccio said:

I went to to find out what it was all about. There wasn't a date on it or anything. I thought it was a tombstone. The paper told the whole story, about how they had a parade, the whole bit. I asked them to put a story in the paper to see if anybody knew anything about it. I went to the Italian clubs and nobody knew anything about it. I finally decided to see if we could just build it.

A committee was soon formed, including Tony DeLucia, Dr. Jim Holton, Manny Stamatakis and Guido Martinelli. We called it Hello Columbus. There were so many people who helped out. The next thing you know we started building the monument. Everybody started stepping in, the commissioners, Representative Holl, Al Panepinto came on board and did the drawing for the monument. He drew the logo for the astronauts.

Alfred Panepinto was indeed a find for the Hello Columbus committee. Panepinto was a world-renowned architect and artist. He had placed second in the design competition in the New York World's Fair in 1938. He was a finalist in London's Crystal Palace International Competition in 1946. He designed several buildings in the Philadelphia area, including those on the campus of Villanova University. Panepinto also designed the logo for NASA's first life sciences space shuttle mission in 1987.

The Columbus Monument sits in a fountain with a half globe coming up out of the water, with the *Santa Maria* sitting atop the globe.

"[Panepinto] said you don't need a picture of Columbus," Ciaccio said. "You have the four elements, the water, the globe, the compass and the ship. That's all you need."

While the monument has fallen into disrepair in recent years, Ciaccio has once again rallied his troops and is currently restoring it.

THE UNDERGROUND RAILROAD

The First Baptist Church, located in Norristown until 1971, was a stop on the Underground Railroad when it was at Airy and Swede Streets, according to *The Underground Railroad* by Charles L. Blockson. Reverend Samuel Aaron was the pastor at First Baptist Church from 1841 to 1844 and invited several abolitionists to speak at the church, including Frederick Douglass and Lucretia Mott. Henry "Box" Brown spoke at the church after his escape. Blockson recalled one particular night at the church when Douglass and Mott left the church arm in arm. Mott was a white woman, and of course, Frederick Douglass, a black man, was one of the most famous abolitionists of his time.

"Norristown was very important in the abolitionist movement. Aaron invited several people to speak at the church," Blockson wrote. "Dan Ross worked with the Corsons. He had a home at the corner of Jacoby and Green. He helped document all of the movements."

Blockson recommends *Reminiscences of the Underground Railroad* by Dr. Hiram Corson for additional reading on the Underground Railroad in our area. Hiram Corson wrote about his brother George Corson and his insatiable appetite for justice. In the book, Corson writes that his brother was born in Plymouth Township in 1803 and spent his entire life as an antislavery advocate. He even opened his home to escaped slaves on the run. Hiram was asked to give a written account of one particular incident and recalled in his book that George had been to visit another of his brothers, Charles, at the "fork of the Skippack and Perkiomen creeks, which would be Lower Providence Township today," and on his way home he came upon a man on horseback who was pulling a colored man with a rope around his neck. The man told him he was his slave and he had every authority to take him wherever he wanted. George Corson made his way to Norristown and waited for the man to arrive. Corson was able to get the man before a justice of the peace, but with the sentiment of the day being mostly proslavery, Corson's pleas for the slave to be released fell on deaf ears. George Corson and his brother Hiram would spend the rest of their days supporting the abolitionist movement.

THE MONTGOMERY COUNTY NORRISTOWN PUBLIC LIBRARY

What once started in a small wooden structure built with $150, the Montgomery County Norristown Public Library now boasts a collection of mammoth proportions and receives tens of thousands of visitors each year.

The library is older than Norristown and is even older than *The Times Herald*. First organized in 1794, the library received its charter in 1796 and began selling shares for $5 each. Members also had to pay $2 a year or could purchase a lifetime membership for $20. For nearly thirty years, the library didn't have a home and was housed by members, until in 1824 $150 was raised to build a structure on Main Street, on a tract of land owned by the Bank of Montgomery County. The small building was erected for a cost of $153.43. It remained there for nearly thirty years, when it was loaded up on a wagon and moved to DeKalb and Penn Streets in 1853. Six years later, the library purchased a piece of property from the First Presbyterian Church and built a new library in the 500 block of DeKalb Street. The library moved a little farther north on DeKalb Street when the First Methodist Church moved to the North End in 1954. At that time, the library also had a branch on Haws Avenue. The library was accredited in 1942 and has maintained steady growth ever since. Today, the library is located at Powell and Swede Streets and has branches throughout Montgomery County.

Meeting minutes from early years revealed some interesting practices at the library. The size of the books was measured when being checked out, and books over a certain size were allowed to be kept longer. Library-goers from out of town could keep their books a week longer than residents in town because it took them longer to make their way back to the library. In one series of minutes, the librarian, who was paid ten dollars a month, asked for a two-dollar raise. The request was debated for four months and eventually denied, although the board at the time decided to allow the librarian to work fewer hours.

Today, meeting minutes contain a brief recounting of some of the more unusual questions the reference department receives, including, "How did the Romans stage their mock naval battles in the Coliseum?" and from another patron who wanted to know the correct spelling of a place in the Philippines called "Nassaboo," where her husband talked about serving during World War II. The reference department successfully determined the place the woman was looking for was Nasugbu, Luzon, Philippines.

BARBADOES ISLAND

Barbadoes Island has a bit of a storied past itself. Known in recent years as the home of the Philadelphia Electric Company's power plant, the island once was home to one of the earliest sporting events in the area. While some of the town's main streets were used for horse racing, Barbadoes Island soon became the equine destination, as racing through the town's streets became somewhat dangerous as the population grew. Jail Lane, which is now Airy Street, was used for horse racing at the time because it had a fence on each side of the street.

An advertisement in the 1804 *Norristown Herald* stated that "Barbadoes Island racing will commence on May 8 when a purse of $400 will be run in a 4-mile heat; the next day, $200 for a three-mile heat; and the third day, $100 for a two-mile heat."

The electric plant was built in 1926 and remained operational until 1997. For more than ten years it has sat dormant. The two smokestacks, which were visible for miles around, were recently torn down. The island is only accessible from a bridge at the foot of Haws Avenue in Norristown.

PART V

MUSINGS FROM THE AUTHOR

As editor of *The Times Herald*, I'm often treated to stories about the history of Norristown. One of the most popular features I've been responsible for starting since coming back to the paper in 2002 is "Days Gone By." We ask our readers to send in photographs from the past, and more often than not, they prompt telephone calls and e-mails from people who know someone in the photograph, or from people who want copies of the photos because their father, grandfather or cousin is in the photograph. The history of Norristown is recorded in the pages of *The Times Herald* and its predecessors. I have been fortunate to sit in the editor's chair here at the thirteenth oldest newspaper in the country. The people I've met and the stories I've been told are enough to fill two, perhaps three volumes on the history of this town. I'm sure I've missed a good deal, so please understand that I consider this only a beginning. Enjoy these final few pages, which include a couple of columns I've written and some correspondence from readers. History never sleeps, and there is always another story to be told.

COLUMN BY COLUMN

The following is a column I wrote after a particularly popular installment of "Days Gone By."

Everyone was known by a nickname in Norristown, the members of the Chicco Beverage basketball team included. *Courtesy of Paul Angelucci.*

IN NORRISTOWN, NICKNAMES MAKE THE MAN

originally published June 20, 2005

When I said the response to the new "Days Gone By" was fantastic, I made a mistake. Fantastic might cover the first couple of weeks we ran the photos, but last week's installment was far and away above fantastic. Extraordinary comes easily to mind. I had about a half dozen telephone calls waiting for me by the time I got to the office Monday morning, and they just kept coming. To refresh your memory just a bit, last week's "Days Gone By" was of the 1947–48 Chicco Beverage basketball team. There were names like Lasorda and Maniscalco and Monestero under the players, but there were a lot of first names missing. Nicknames were plentiful, though, and that seemed to be what caught most people's attention.

"Popeye" Carpani is the brother of "Sunday" DeAngelis. Sunday told me that Popeye's first name is really Dominic, as did a lot of other people who called in, but there's nothing like getting it right from one of his siblings. By the way, Sunday said that Popeye never did like the nickname Popeye.

"Muffy's" son, Mike Maniscalco, dropped me an e-mail and told me that his father's first name is Frank. Thanks, Mike, I do appreciate it. Mike also told me that the Mike Maniscalco in the picture is his uncle.

There were a lot of people who called to give me some help, but none more so than Theresa Dippolito. Theresa is the wife of the late coach of the team, Alex "Jinks" Dippolito. She had the lowdown on everyone and a story or two to tell. I told her I was fascinated with the nicknames and she just said, "Stan, no one knew anyone's first names, everyone was known by their nickname."

Other people just called to tell me how much they enjoyed the photos and the memories they brought back. Dante Volpe recalled his days at Valley Forge Military Academy, where he said Harry Lasorda would bring him zeps from Norristown.

Lynn DeGiacomo called to tell me that the unidentified man in that photo was actually her brother, Paul Gillette, and that he was about seventeen years old at the time. Thanks Lynn, I want to get as many people identified in the photos as possible.

Remember, I'm looking for photographs with people in them. I like the team photos a lot, but you can send regular crowd shots as well. We don't always have to know who everyone is in the picture. Someone asked about some photographs they have of downtown Norristown. We have dozens of those in our archives. I want people, real people like we've had in the past couple of weeks. "Days Gone By" doesn't mean they have to be forgotten days.

One of the young men in the Chicco Beverage basketball team photo that was only briefly mentioned in the column above was a kid called Mungo. Most of the rest of the world knows him as Tommy Lasorda.

The "Days Gone By" feature in *The Times Herald* continues to be very popular. One of our more recent photos was of the 1940 Royal Ravens softball team that included Ed Slanker, Ray Bosler, Joe Kirkpatrick, Frank Slanker, Harold Beiderman, Ray Hartenstine, Earl Armitage, Bob Williams, Ralph Kinckner, Paul Westhafer, Bill Fritz, Don Williams and Frank Andrews.

Another column that garnered quite a response was on the topic of trolleys, which have a rich history in Norristown.

TROLLEY KEEPS THINGS ROLLING ALONG

originally published February 21, 2005

I was talking about slowing things down a bit so the column would be much more enjoyable and, it is hoped, mistake free. I'm really going to slow down this week and continue along with the trolley ride.

For such a small entry, my mention of the trolley tracks under Markley Street in Norristown sure did elicit a large response. Rick Brown wrote in to tell me about the Ridge Pike trolley, built in 1896, that ended at the foot of Mile Hill in Lower Providence. Rick said the trolley company built a park at the end of the line and—here's a new one for me—"flannelgraph artists" entertained.

The line was later extended all the way to Reading. If you drive through Collegeville, you'll see the PowerHouse flea market. The PowerHouse provided the juice to keep that trolley running, as did the Pechin Mill in Lower Providence. Thanks, Rick. Now all I have to do is figure out what the heck a "flannelgraph" is.

Jack Kowal, Bridgeport's very own district justice, called to tell me that the trolley I was talking about last week started at Main and Swede Streets at the Philadelphia and Western depot. That's where the new DEP building is. The builders saved the front of the old depot so you can still see it when you're driving through town. Jack was the first of many people to tell me the line that went up Markley Street to Allentown was called the Liberty Bell line.

Phil Smith, a Norristown train aficionado, confirmed the Liberty Bell name. Phil also told me that the Lehigh Valley Traction Co. operated the line.

I did a little research into the flannelgraph phenomenon (it's been a couple of days since I started this column), and I was chastised by a Web site in the process. The page started with something like, "Anyone who attended Sunday school during the past four or five decades has experienced flannelgraph or just wasn't paying attention."

Apparently, I wasn't paying attention.

A flannelgraph is a depiction of a Bible scene on, obviously, flannel. The flannelgraphs were used to make teaching the Bible fun for kids in Sunday school. Thanks Rick, but I still don't remember them.

Rather than bore you with a dry recounting of the history of the Liberty Bell, the following are excerpts from a letter received from a reader after the above column appeared in *The Times Herald* with a firsthand account of memories of the famed trolley.

Musings from the Author

Dear Stan,

I took notice of your interest in the Norristown area trolley lines in your column the other week, to which several readers have responded. I thought maybe I could add to your "stash" of information, especially of that pertaining to the Lehigh Valley Transit Company, better known as the Liberty Bell Route. Many historians believe the trolley line somewhat reflected the route taken when moving the Liberty Bell from Philadelphia to Allentown for safety reasons during the time the British had occupied Philadelphia during the Revolutionary War.

I fondly recall as a young lad of 4 or 5 years of age growing up in Souderton during the mid 1940s, when my mother and I would take the trolley to Lansdale to shop. During that same period, my parents owned a dry cleaning business in Sellersville and we would take the LVT on days when my mother would go in to help.

But my most memorable trips were those to Norristown when my mother wanted to do some "serious" shopping. I always looked forward to those excursions because I knew we would be having lunch at the soda fountain counter at either Woolworths or Grants, department stores long gone from the Norristown landscape.

After living in West Point several years, another village served by the LVT, we moved to Norristown in 1951 and my long trolley rides ended, although I still enjoyed watching the brightly colored cream and red trolleys running up and down Markley Street. However, this excitement didn't last long because it was later that same year when the entire trolley experience vanished from the scene when the Liberty Bell line was abandoned. I can remember as a sixth grader at Roosevelt Elementary School watching out the window as the tracks were ripped up, ending a fabulous part of eastern Pennsylvania transportation history.

Only one of the Liberty Bell trolleys escaped the scrap yard. Number 1030 car was loaded on a flat rail car and shipped to Maine. The car was completely restored and today operates for fan trips at the Seashore Trolley Museum at Kennebunkport. Someday I hope to make the trip to Kennebunkport and take a nostalgic trip on Number 1030, a current photo of which I've enclosed.

Another popular landmark of the Liberty Bell Route was the bridge spanning Main Street with its recognizable clock. The bridge allowed passengers to transfer to the P&W Line and continue on to Philadelphia.

One of the few remaining structures of the LVT is located at DeKalb Pike and Township Line Road in East Norriton. The brick building was an electrical substation for the line. It later became a hardware store and currently is a beauty salon.

Sincerely,
Bob Landes

The Liberty Bell #1030 car is still on display at the museum and is only brought out for special occasions, according to Roger Tobin, a caretaker at the museum. Mr. Tobin was nice enough to pass along my request for more information on exactly how #1030 made its way to their museum.

A few weeks later, Edward L. Ramsdell, librarian for the New England Electric Railway Historical Society, sent me a description of the car and its acquisition:

SE DT AR High Speed Lightweight Interurban Parlor Car
Builder: American Car & Foundry 1931
Indiana Railroad 1931–1940; Lehigh Valley Transit Co. 1940–1951
Accessioned 1951—#V1-51.1.1

The first item of possible interest is a memo-to-file written in 2001 by Ben Minnich, at that time Manager of Collection Development. He states "This first car to come to Seashore from outside of New England was one of a fleet commissioned by the Indiana Railroad's Bowman Elder in a bid to save the system. This car was sold to LVT along with several from the Cincinnati and Lake Erie Railway (C&LE) to update the LVT's Liberty Bell Service between Philadelphia and Allentown." He noted that there was great concern among the museum's leadership when LVT suddenly abandoned interurban service and it seemed that all the cars would be scrapped. He travelled to New York and Allentown to attempt to acquire a car. He finally purchased the car for $1,000 and, 1030 being the most desirable, he picked it out at the Allentown carhouse. Its trucks and motors had already been sold so another set was transferred over from one of the C&LE cars, C&LE car 1002, car 1002 was the car featured in the famous airplane-interurban race in 1930.

One of the museum's founders, Theodore F. Santarelli, and another member went down and arranged for loading and rail shipment of the car to the MTA Shops in Everett, MA where it sat for some months before being trucked to Maine. Four museum members went to Allentown the last week of January 1952 and loaded car 1030 onto PM flat #16603 (Pere Marquette Rwy.). The car actually left Allentown on Friday February 8 and arrived Sunday at the Beacon Park Yards of the Boston & Albany. It was delivered to the MTA Everett Shops on monday and unloaded on tuesday. It rested there, and was worked on by museum members, until December of 1952 when it was moved by highway to Kennebunkport. With major and ongoing financial support from the Lehigh Valley Chapter of the National Railway Historical Society restoration, first of the exterior and roof and then to return the car to its parlor car configuration (LVT had reconfigured it to a standard coach arrangement), went forward through 1976. Interior furniture and carpeting was obtained from various businesses in the Allentown area, both through purchase and generous donation. The car was the highlight of an open house held on October 9–10, 1976 at Seashore. In the early '90s the car was repainted and certain mechanical repairs were undertaken. Also in the mid-90s a railroad historian arranged for the donation of the original motors of 1030 that had been sold at the time of LVT's ceasing interurban operations. These motors were placed in storage at the time as the substitute Westinghouse motors obtained in 1952 were performing satisfactorily.

A Paper Trail

This book just wouldn't be complete without taking you on a journey through the history of *The Times Herald*. From its humble beginnings as the *Norristown Gazette* in a Main Street print shop to its sprawling plant at Markley and Ann Streets, *The Times Herald* has survived two centuries of human triumphs and tragedies to remain one of the longest-running newspapers in the country.

The Times Herald has chronicled the events of the past 210 years as we moved from horse and buggies on dirt roads to custom cars on superhighways, from merely gazing at the heavens to exploring them close up, and from the hand-to-hand combat of the Civil War to high-powered air attacks overseas. *The Times Herald* has lived through every American president since George Washington, whose obituary ran in the *Gazette* during its first year of publication in 1799.

It all started in a downtown print shop on Egypt Street (now Main Street) 210 years ago. David Sower and a small group of accomplices printed the

Only one of the Liberty Bell trolleys escaped the scrap yard. Number 1030 car was loaded on a flat railcar and shipped to Maine. The car was completely restored and today operates for fan trips at the Seashore Trolley Museum at Kennebunkport.

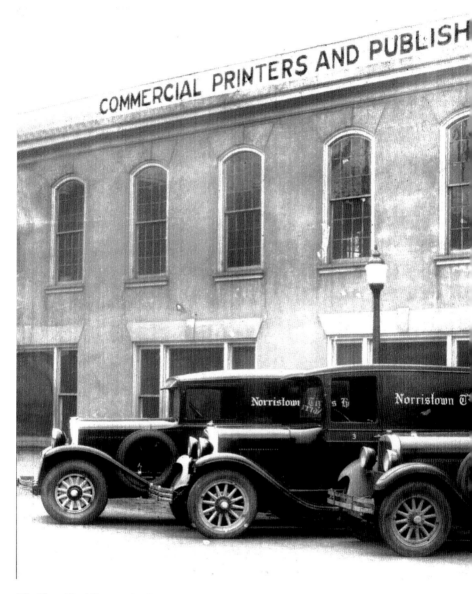

The Times Herald has survived two centuries of human triumphs and tragedies to remain one of the longest continually publishing newspapers in the country.

first copy of the *Norristown Gazette* on June 15, 1799. David Sower was a son of Christopher Sower, a preacher and controversial publisher. Christopher Sower, who advocated peace and disdained war, was a bishop in the Church of the Brethren. For publishing his antiwar sentiments, Christopher Sower

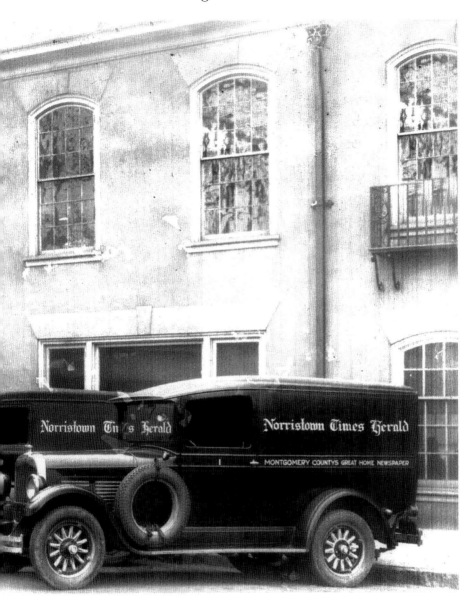

was branded a "Tory," a derogatory term used to describe Americans who were loyal to the British during the American Revolution. Stripped of his possessions and fearing for his life, Christopher Sower fled Norristown and earned a meager living as a bookbinder.

His son David, a bookseller and bookbinder as well, printed a prototype of the *Norristown Gazette* on June 1, 1799. Positive response from residents prompted Sower to publish the official first edition of the *Gazette* on June 15.

In its first year of publication, the *Gazette* had just four pages with three columns of print on each page. But it was enough to spawn an institution that has outlasted nearly every other industry of the eighteenth century.

In 1800, the name of the *Gazette* was changed to the *Norristown Herald and Weekly Advertiser*, a name it retained in various forms until 1922, when it was merged with the *Norristown Daily Times* to create the *Norristown Times Herald*. But during those 121 years, the *Herald* went through many changes.

In 1808, Charles Sower, oldest son of David Sr., bought the *Norristown Herald and Weekly Advertiser*. The Main Street building where the *Gazette* began in 1799 was sold soon after.

In 1816, David Sower Jr., son of *Gazette* founder David Sr., purchased the *Norristown Herald* and served as editor and publisher for eighteen years. During his tenure, David Jr. enlarged the pages and added a significant amount of office equipment. At some point he changed the name of the paper to the *Norristown Herald and Montgomery county Advertiser*. And yes, the "c" in county was lowercased.

On December 15, 1829, the *Free Press* was started by Henry S. Bell.

In 1854, David Sower sold the *Norristown Herald* to John Hodgson of Doylestown. Hodgson built a stone building on Main Street below DeKalb to house the offices of the *Norristown Herald*.

In 1837, *Free Press* owner Robert Iredell bought the *Norristown Herald and Weekly Advertiser*. The first *Norristown Herald and Free Press* was published February 1, 1837.

On March 1, 1864, Morgan E. Wills and Robert Iredell Jr. became proprietors of the *Norristown Herald and Free Press*. In October 1864, the *Norristown Republican* was consolidated with the *Norristown Herald and Free Press*, and Howard M. Jenkins became proprietor. Jenkins retired in 1866.

On May 19, 1869, the partnership of Wills and Iredell was dissolved, and on December 20, 1869, Wills established the *Daily Herald* as sole proprietor. The paper remained the property of Wills's estate following his death in 1908.

In 1881, the *Norristown Daily Times* was founded by Captain William Rennyson of Bridgeport, a Civil War veteran with no newspaper experience. Publishing out of a second-floor office above an East Main Street store, the paper crusaded for public improvements.

In November 1921, Ralph Beaver Strassburger bought the *Daily Herald*, and in June 1922, the paper moved to its current location on Markley Street

Upper Merion icon Ed Dybicz was home on leave during World War II and was captured on film reading the *Times Herald*. *Courtesy of Ed Dybicz*.

at the Airy Street bridge. On December 26, 1922, Strassburger's purchase of the *Norristown Daily Times* was announced. A week later, the *Herald* and *Times* were merged. Strassburger established the *Norristown Times Herald*, later renamed *The Times Herald*, as a local institution. The Strassburger era lasted until 1993, when, following the death of owner J.A. Peter Strassburger on April 20, 1993, his estate sold the newspaper to the Journal Register Company of Trenton, New Jersey. In December 1993, *The Times Herald* began publishing as a morning edition and a new offset press was installed to replace the letterpress that had printed the *Herald* since the 1950s.

In March 1994, the first Sunday edition of *The Times Herald* was published.

During the past two hundred years, more than seventy-two thousand editions have been published, with only a few minor glitches. On July 14, 1931, the *Herald* suffered a substantial delay when floodwaters swamped the entire first floor, and on October 24, 1968, an equipment breakdown delayed distribution by several hours as couriers traveled more than one hundred miles to deliver replacement parts while *The Times Herald* pressroom crew rewired out-of-use equipment. On July 18, 2006, a major storm hit the area, causing a power outage at the printing plant. The paper wasn't printed until late the next day, instead of its regular deadline, but the papers hit the streets with the July 19, 2006 date intact. On all three occasions, the *Herald* upheld the long-standing newspaper tradition of "getting the paper out" no matter what adversity is presented because its readers and advertisers have come to rely on it.

I was at the helm during the July 18, 2006 power outage. There simply was no way I was going to be the first editor in the paper's two-hundred-year history who didn't put out a paper. It was close, but around 8:30 p.m., my publisher, Shelley Meenan, and I grabbed the keys to a *Times Herald* van and headed to Bucks County, where we had convinced a printer to put us on their press. We came back about an hour and a half later and there were carriers and managers waiting for us at the loading dock. Home delivery made it out the door, and we even managed to get a few papers into the local stores.

Being the editor of the paper of record for Norristown, I find myself in a unique position. History is very important to the residents of Norristown, and we have been very diligent in documenting that history since the days before the "Biggest Borough in the World" was even established.

I hope you have enjoyed the journey through these pages.

ABOUT THE AUTHOR

S tan Huskey is a resident of West Norriton Township, which originally was part of the Williamstadt Manor that William Penn Jr. sold to Isaac Norris. Stan is the editor of *The Times Herald*, a daily newspaper based in Norristown, covering central Montgomery County, Pennsylvania. He has garnered a number of writing awards throughout his career, including a 2008 First Place Award for column writing from the Pennsylvania Associated Press Managing Editors Association. He is a member of the Norristown Rotary Club Board of Directors and also sits on the board of the Montgomery County Norristown Public Library. He also sits on the Montgomery County District Attorney's Ad Hoc Committee for Minority Relations as well as the Montgomery County Sheriff's Citizen Advisory Council.

Visit us at
www.historypress.net